More Advance Praise for *The CEO and the Monk*

"*The CEO and the Monk* is anything but a traditional 'business book'—it is an inspiration! Given the fine example herein, there's no reason every company cannot be run in the same ethical and spiritual way."

> —Dr. Ian Mitroff, Distinguished Professor of
> Business Policy at the University of Southern
> California, founder of the USC Center for
> Crisis Management, and author of *A Spiritual
> Audit of Corporate America*

"Breaking through the clutter of both the self-aggrandizing tales of CEO bravado and the growing piles of books on CEO scandals, *The CEO and the Monk* reminds us that leadership still matters in forging the character of an enterprise and its people. It leaves platitudes behind and takes the reader into the mind of the CEO to wrestle with the gripping backstage drama of real choices that challenge the soul of the firm and the reputation of its leadership. I look at dozens of management books each month, and rarely is such candor and insight offered."

> —Jeffrey Sonnenfeld, Associate Dean, Yale School
> of Management

"*The CEO and the Monk* takes you inside the soul of one company and two men to demonstrate how integrity leads to corporate profitability and personal fulfillment. Read this book to experience the pain and joy of how two perspectives can merge to create a workplace that serves as an opportunity for financial and personal growth."

> —Mark Albion, author of the *New York Times*
> Business Bestseller, *Making a Life, Making a Living*®

"Catell and Moore have fought for the very soul of business—and won! They hold to their beliefs that a balance sheet should be informed by the human condition, and built upon dignity, grace, and humor. *The CEO and the Monk* is a powerful and wonderful testament to doing the right thing—every day. Read it slowly, digest it, and profit from these prophets!"

> —Bill Jensen, former Brooklynite and author of
> *Simplicity* and *Work 2.0*

"Captivating, interesting, and helpful . . . *The CEO and the Monk* gives all of us who transact business something to think about."

> —Monsignor Tom Hartman, co-host and co-author
> of the "God Squad" national TV talk show
> and syndicated newspaper column, and
> an Emmy Award-winning director

"Thank you, Bob Catell and Kenny Moore, for reminding all of us that even in our wounded world it is still possible to do well by doing good."

> —Rabbi Marc Gellman, Ph.D., co-host
> and co-author of the "God Squad" national
> TV talk show and syndicated newspaper column

"*The CEO and the Monk* is a good read for any corporate executive, particularly in today's troubled corporate environment. It shows time and again the importance of maintaining a moral compass in the executive suite and staying in touch with the thinking of all employees. At the core of the book is how these principles helped Bob Catell, with help from his corporate ombudsman, steer his way successfully through Brooklyn Union's merger with LILCO to form KeySpan. I enjoyed this book thoroughly."

> —David W. Heleniak, Senior Partner,
> Shearman & Sterling LLP

"We need more compassionate and caring leaders like Kenny Moore and Bob Catell. The stories in this inspiring book are proof that enlightened organizations exist and are making a difference in the world."

> —Judi Neal, Ph.D., Director, Center for Spirit
> at Work, University of New Haven

"*The CEO and the Monk* make an extraordinary team—the power of their purpose is absolutely contagious. This book is a gem."

> —Richard J. Leider, founder of The Inventure
> Group and best-selling author of *Repacking
> Your Bags* and *The Power of Purpose*

The CEO and the Monk

The CEO
and the Monk

One Company's Journey
to Profit and Purpose

ROBERT B. CATELL AND KENNY MOORE
WITH GLENN RIFKIN

WILEY

John Wiley & Sons, Inc.

Published by John Wiley & Sons, Inc., Hoboken, New Jersey.
Published simultaneously in Canada.

For general information on our other products and services please contact our Customer Care Department within the United States at (800) 762-2974, outside the United States at (317) 572-3993 or fax (317) 572-4002.

Wiley also publishes its books in a variety of electronic formats. Some content that appears in print may not be available in electronic books. For more information about Wiley products, visit our web site at www.wiley.com.

Library of Congress Cataloging-in-Publication Data:

Catell, Robert B.
    The CEO and the monk : one company's journey to profit and purpose / Robert B. Catell and Kenny Moore with Glenn Rifkin.
        p.   cm.
    ISBN 0-471-45011-1 (cloth)
    1. KeySpan Corporation—History.   2. Energy industries—United States—History.   I. Moore, Kenny.   II. Rifkin, Glenn.   III. Title.
    HD9502.U54K483   2004
    333.79'0973—dc22   2003020247

Printed in the United States of America.

10 9 8 7 6 5 4 3 2 1

To my mother,
For a lifetime of inspiration and love; for teaching me how to see the world and to do the right thing.

—RBC

To the fair and beautiful Cynthia,
Who has rescued me from monasticism, nurtured me through cancer, schooled me in the etiquette of corporate politics (still much work to do here . . .), and blessed my life with children, marital bliss, and a spirit of compassion.

—KCM

Contents

◦～

INTRODUCTION

~

What Is Good for the Soul Is Also Good for Business

Business is, in the end, a moral matter.

—Charles Handy

In March 2001, Jeffrey Skilling, the president and CEO of Enron Corporation, addressed an overflow gathering at the Goldman Sachs energy industry analysts meeting in Aspen, Colorado. A brash, young former McKinsey consultant, Skilling had played a key role in transforming Enron into a fast-moving corporate steamroller. Enron had become one of the world's biggest corporations, a dominant behemoth in the energy industry intent on crushing competition and changing the rules of the game.

Under Skilling and Enron chairman Kenneth Lay, Enron had moved away from the traditional energy supply business model and begun to trade energy as a commodity. Using technology and a smart, aggressive workforce, Enron had emerged, in Skilling's modest opinion, as the "new paradigm," the model of the twenty-first-century corporate juggernaut. By way of a videotape, he told the audience members that day that "the big oil companies are dinosaurs. The energy merchants and the telecommunications giants are going to take over the world. Because Enron has the systems and the people, there's no reason that we won't become the world's biggest company."

He added that the new winning strategy was an "asset light" strategy. You didn't have to own assets, you just had to control the assets, he stated. His implication was that if energy companies continued in their roles as traditional suppliers of gas and services, they would soon become obsolete. The future was for those who forsook capital-intensive fixed assets like pipelines and power plants and focused instead on creating markets. Inside Enron's take-no-prisoners workplace, 20,000 intensely competitive employees were pushing the proverbial envelope further and further. To those listening and watching the stock market, there seemed little that could slow Enron down.

The audience sat in stunned silence. This kind of hubris was more than a bit unusual in the energy industry. In the audience that day was Robert Catell, the chairman and CEO of KeySpan Corporation. Like his industry counterparts, Catell had been watching Enron's exploits and had grown worried that Skilling might be right. The whole financial world had been turned on its head in the past few years. Tiny start-ups with little more than a business plan filed initial public offerings (IPOs) and in a few short months had market capitalizations larger than that of General Motors. Prognosticators were crowing that the Internet would change business dramatically and forever. Stock options had spawned millionaires and billionaires on an almost daily basis. The old rules were being tossed out the window in favor of New Economy standards. How could KeySpan, a successful but conservative and traditional energy company, hope to compete with the likes of Enron?

KeySpan is a publicly traded $6 billion, Brooklyn, New York–based energy company with 12,000 employees in New York and New England. It is one of the largest energy companies in the populous Northeast and the fifth largest natural gas distributor in the United States, but compared to Enron, it was a turtle plodding along in the dust of a very fast rabbit.

In early 2001, it was hard to be a turtle. All around, the world seemed to have changed overnight. There were signs that the Internet bubble was finally about to burst, but no one was quite sure what the future held. Catell, however concerned by Skilling's view of the energy industry, refused to panic or to react impetuously. In his heart, something about Enron didn't feel right. The model was sketchy at the edges, replete with countless unanswered questions. It all looked too easy, too good to be true. Catell had been in the energy industry for more than 40 years, and he understood viscerally the bones of the business, having worked out in the streets of Brooklyn where the pipes are laid and customer expectations are born.

As the result of the merger of several utility companies, including Brooklyn Union Gas, a local company that had been a fixture in Brooklyn for more than a century, Keyspan was, if anything, the antithesis of Enron. It was a company deeply ingrained in the community, a place where one generation after another came to work and to which customers felt a deep, abiding loyalty.

Even if Catell had a moment's itch to emulate Enron, he knew that KeySpan was not that kind of company and he was not that kind of leader. His doubts were fleeting. He left the Goldman Sachs meeting with a resolve that KeySpan was already on the right road and that there was plenty to get done regardless of what happened with Enron. He had learned a long time ago that there was remarkable strength in staying a steady course and doing the right thing.

Of course, Enron's remarkable implosion is already the stuff of business legend. Within just months of that meeting, Skilling abruptly resigned and the collapse of Enron made global headlines. In the years since that meeting, so much has happened that Skilling's proclamation of Enron as potentially the world's largest company now seems like an empty whisper from a surreal past. In fact, in the aftermath of a series of cataclysmic events, both beyond and within the world of business, it is crucial to step back and consider where things are and where they might be going. The staggering events of September 11th, the continuing economic slide, the anxiety-provoking war against terrorism, the war in Iraq, and the widespread impact of corporate greed and malfeasance have rocked the business world in ways not seen since the Great Depression and the onset of World War II.

Sometimes, in the midst of such great trauma, there is tremendous value in seeking out the smaller, subtler, yet far more profound stories that continue to fuel the hope and inspiration that is the foundation of American business. This book tells one of those stories.

Though it is ostensibly a story about business, it is more than that. It is about a journey that circles along the arc of a company, through its leaders, its employees, its customers, and its core beliefs.

Remarkably, in this new millennium business environment, the KeySpan story is not about scandal, avarice, or the dramatic misplacement of trust and integrity (though the company has survived its own bout with executive greed and scandal). Instead, it is a story about relationships and attitudes, individuals and communities, risks taken in the name of possibility. It is about "enlightened self-interest" and the notion that leadership that embraces a set of higher values can simultaneously reap priceless goodwill as well as profits.

It is about two men whose career paths could not have been more different but whose lives converged and intersected in a moment of grace and serendipity. Within the staid and arcane world of an energy utility, a former engineer who rose through the corporate ranks all the way to the chief executive suite found an unlikely ally: a former priest who had lived a monastic life for 15 years before forsaking the Church to enter the very foreign and daunting corporate environment. Together, the pair has built upon long-held corporate values to fashion a different kind of workplace, a workplace where spirituality is woven into the fabric of daily life without religious overtones but loaded with meaning.

In most ways, KeySpan is, in fact, a corporate entity like most others. The company worries about making money and satisfying its stakeholders. Like other utilities, KeySpan has undergone wrenching change in the face of deregulation, a controversial merger, and a volatile business climate. It isn't always as profitable or fast moving as its officers and employees would like. But something happens inside KeySpan that spawns an atmosphere that most companies quietly yearn for but struggle to achieve. Without fanfare, KeySpan has embraced a management philosophy that somehow balances bottom-line demands with a sense of caring and family. There is the palpable belief in the proposition that what is good for the soul is also good for business. Though it may sound like New Age folderol, the truth is evident throughout the company and illustrated by the actions of the CEO and the monk.

Robert B. Catell, chief executive officer at KeySpan since 1991, has overseen the transformation of a small Brooklyn gas company into one of the nation's largest and most successful energy companies. He is a soft-spoken, self-effacing leader, a 45-year KeySpan/Brooklyn Union veteran, whose gentle, common-man persona belies a tough, cerebral competence that has held the company together through more than a decade of turbulence.

Kenny Moore is the former monk with the title of "corporate ombudsman," a position created for him by Bob Catell. Kenny reports directly to Catell and roams the company freely, listening to the concerns of both employees and executives while "engaging the soul of the company," as he likes to put it. His role is to help foster corporate change in a time of difficult transformation and to infuse the agenda with a sense of spiritual connectedness. Though he now operates in concrete and glass towers rather than hallowed halls with stained-glass windows and wooden pews, he feels that his mandate remains much the same.

Corporate journeys are complex, interconnecting paths experienced from myriad points of view. For Bob Catell and Kenny Moore, the journey is about creating an environment and establishing a legacy that differentiates KeySpan in many ways. What is different about KeySpan is difficult to define. Perhaps it is a commitment to doing the right thing—turning over important conservation land to the state rather than opting for development; using social workers to help low-income customers sift through their financial burdens; encouraging a former monk to retain his role as a confidant, mentor, and teacher without the trappings of religion.

Perhaps it is the recognition that employees bring all their baggage to work. Sitting in front of you is not just a professional individual but that person's entire family, their biases, their strengths. Employees have chosen to come to this workplace, and thus it becomes a community in which people spend a majority of their waking hours. Somehow, under Catell, the company recognizes that it must reach people on not only a professional level but also on an emotional level and a personal level. With Kenny Moore's help, Catell has touched the people of KeySpan in a meaningful, even powerful way. Not everyone feels the touch or accepts it. There are skeptics, as there are in every organization. For some, it may seem too New Age, too uncomfortable.

But for most, the message is well received, even cherished. It crosses lines: men and women, operations people and white-collar executives, management staff and union workers. In a time of widespread disenchantment with corporate America, these people feel an undiminished pride in where they work, a sense of belonging and loyalty that has become passé in most organizations. In a time when CEOs are doing "perp walks" in handcuffs before news cameras, KeySpan's success is testimony both to the universality of the message and to the resolve and belief on the part of the CEO that the message is an essential ingredient in the makeup of the company.

KeySpan is not the most exciting company for which to work. It is, after all, a utility, an energy company that is dominated by an engineering culture. What attracts people to KeySpan is that at its core, in its Brooklyn heritage, is the feeling of family, like a gathering of aunts and uncles and cousins from Canarsie, Bay Ridge, Marine Park, and Flatbush. Its roots are humble, middle-class, unpretentious. And though its leaders are smart, savvy, and focused on profits and shareholder value, they are respectful of this quality that has endured difficult and trying transitions. This is the vision that Bob Catell has driven with passion and commitment since he became CEO. This is what he is determined to hold onto even as the company grows, expands into new regions, and struggles with its own transformation.

You may not find any solutions to your own corporate angst in the KeySpan story. But the best lessons tend to appear in the least expected places, perhaps even a gas company in the heart of Brooklyn.

The CEO

~

I can't remember the first time I met Kenny Moore. But when I got a chance to get to know him a bit, I realized that he had something more to bring to the company than traditional business skills. The fact that he had lived a monastic life in the priesthood for 15 years and had left to find his way in the world of business was intriguing. The fact that he had also survived a life-threatening bout with cancer, serious "terminal" cancer, and had recovered and returned to the company more energized than before also struck me.

But what really caught my attention, after a few meetings in which we got to know each other, was how strong his feelings were about people and how you can get things done by knowing people and working with people and listening to people. He expressed an intuitive sense of the goodness in people and the ability to connect and touch that goodness that rang true to me and the values I had been brought up with.

It was the early 1990s. I had not been the CEO of Brooklyn Union Gas for very long at that time and I was trying to figure out how I was going to make my mark on this company. What would I do differently? We had been this wonderful little local gas company for nearly 100 years. We had not only established a reputation as a good, reliable supplier of gas to our customers in Brooklyn, Staten Island, and Queens, but we had become an integral part of the community. We were good corporate citizens. Customers loved us. Brooklyn loved us. Employees were proud to work for us, and it was a badge of honor to say you worked at Brooklyn Union. We were steady and solid, profitable and philanthropic, popular with regulators and politicians and union leaders.

But in the early 1990s, I began to see the nature of our industry changing. We were slowly but surely moving from a very tightly regulated monopoly to a much more competitive, unregulated environment. Changes were coming, and it would be up to me to lead the company head-on into this new era. We had a significant challenge ahead of us to maintain that close, what we called "family" relationship with our employees and customers and yet operate in a much more competitive marketplace.

I knew we had the business skills to navigate through these changes. But I believed that we needed something that would help our employees experience the changes—changes that could and would be hard and even traumatic—in a positive way. I wanted to find a way to capture what was good about the old Brooklyn Union and keep it alive in whatever kind of company we would become. I felt that Kenny could provide a mechanism to help me do that. In our discussions, Kenny talked about the employees and the passion. We discussed ways in which I could reach out through him and really capture that passion.

This was more than a business issue, though business issues will always lurk nearby when you are talking about a publicly held company. This was about spirituality and doing the right thing. It had nothing to do with religion even though Kenny was steeped in that tradition. I saw Kenny as a representation of the "soul" of the company, even if that sounds a bit corny. If I was going to lead this company through the next decade and into the new millennium, I felt strongly that we needed to build a company that had more than just a business perspective. I'd always felt that if I had the opportunity to become chief executive, I wanted to lead a company that had heart, that had an agenda that went beyond profits and losses and share price on Wall Street.

My feelings about our employees stemmed from lessons I learned early in life. I had been raised by my mother in the Borough Park section of Brooklyn. My parents had gotten divorced when I was very young and then my father died soon after. My mother raised my sister and me alone. We never thought of ourselves as poor, but we had little money. What we had was a tremendous amount of love in our home. We also had stern guidance from my mother, who taught me early on about working and earning money and taking responsibility.

And my mother taught me a lot about people. She loved people and had many friends. Her friends were of all races and nationalities. Our apartment, small as it was, was always filled with fascinating people of various ethnic and religious backgrounds and even varied sexual preferences. I got a good dose of diversity long before that term became politically correct. She didn't care about race, creed, or color. What she cared about was whether you were a good person. She was quite outspoken and very strong-willed and remains so at age 96. Her behavior made a deep and lasting impression on me, and it had a lot to do with shaping my relationships with people. I honestly respect people, all kinds of people. I believe that everyone has something to offer and to be proud of. My mother instilled in me that people matter and that it is important to do the right thing.

In that regard, Kenny and I connected at the right time. I saw something in his dealings with people that went well beyond the usual human resources role. It seemed to me he brought a different perspective, a more human touch that warmed the cold business relationship for employees. I felt good in my meetings with him. The exchanges we had were frank, honest, and direct. He had no personal agenda that interfered with his ability to make a real connection with me or whomever he was talking with. There was something there, I thought, and if we could grow that inside the company, it would be a good thing. And that's when I decided we should create a special role for Kenny, a unique position, which we later formalized as the corporate ombudsman. Though he would still technically be part of human resources, he would report directly to me.

What I sought, more than anything, was to have Kenny serve as a conduit between me and the company population. We were going to be heading into turbulence, and I wanted someone out there who would provide insight to me, unfiltered and unfettered communication that I could trust. The CEO often gets filtered information. People tell him what they think he wants to hear. We have 12,000 employees in New York, New Jersey, and New England, and as much as I am out and around the company, I can't be everywhere and hear everyone. I wanted to know what people were really thinking and feeling. I said to Kenny, "You go out there and be my eyes and ears in the company." I wasn't looking for a corporate spy or informant. There would be no confidences divulged. I wasn't going to confront someone who offered a negative view.

Rather, Kenny would present the issues he encountered and offer suggestions on how I could respond to them. I knew there would be skeptics and naysayers who would openly question Kenny's role. I believed that Kenny could handle that and eventually convert them. Still, I am amazed how often he has won over the cynics. It isn't an easy role to fill, and it takes a special kind of human being to walk the line that he walks. His work inside the company has been quiet, unassuming, and astounding. He really has made a difference.

The past decade has been rewarding and profitable for me, for our employees and shareholders, and for this company. We have grown and spread ourselves into new businesses and new territories. We have encountered daunting obstacles along the way and overcome most of them to keep moving forward.

As an energy utility, we don't have the luxury to sit back and think about our future very often. We are on call 24 hours a day, seven days a week. We have to create the future while the present swirls around us.

Working together with Kenny, I have been able to hold onto the values I learned from my mother and from 45 years at this company. We've commingled our visions about profits and purpose. I wish we had a formula we could offer and a blueprint for success. We don't. This is our journey and our story. You might read this and decide to go out and hire a retired monk. Or better yet, you might just consider how simple it is to find the soul within your own organization if you just start looking.

The Monk

*I*n 1982, after spending 15 years in a monastic community as a Catholic priest, I decided it was time to leave. Like many others who have made promises they ultimately could not keep, I came to personally understand the counsel of Tennessee Williams: "There is a time for departure even when there's no certain place to go."

I returned to live with my widowed mother in a one-bedroom apartment in New York City. In leaving the religious life, what I had hoped for were privacy, time for reflection, and more independence. What I got were cramped quarters, a protective mother, and more personal poverty than I experienced as a monk. My desire was to be on my own. But I still had not attained the freedom I sought. Eventually, a divine insight was presented: What I truly needed was a job and some money! This proved to be no easy task for one whose sole credentials were an advanced degree in theology, a deep spiritual life, and a propensity for burning incense.

My job search eventually brought me to Brooklyn Union Gas and a rising executive named Bob Catell. I accepted a position in the human resources department and prepared to enter corporate America and leave my religious traditions behind. Or so I thought.

Much to my surprise, the skills of the monastery had a place in the business world. Employee surveys increasingly confront executives with three major issues: nobody trusts their supervisors; employees don't believe in senior management; and workers are too stressed out to care. Problems with trust, belief, and caring. In my monastic days, we referred to this self-same quandary as a crisis of faith, hope, and charity.

I began to discover that the problems confronting business leaders were not only fiscal, they were also spiritual. And, as Divine Providence would have it, all this took on practical meaning when I came face-to-face with Bob Catell. He was a hard-nosed corporate executive with a soul; a person equally at home with corporate profit and with individual purpose; a businessman who longed to manage the "soft" side of the business as aggressively as he managed its hard side.

He was also a man with a mission. The staid world of utilities was being forced to transform itself into an industry of nimble, deregulated energy companies. That would require significant change. It would mean taking a company on a journey from security and complacency into an unknown future, fraught with uncertainty and danger, all with the positive prospects of a future promised land.

Like Moses of the Old Testament, Bob needed to move a large group of people out of their present homeland into a desert experience of pain and risk, holding out the hope of a future place flowing with milk and honey. The priest in me understood how formidable this challenge would be. The business side of me realized that Bob could not accomplish this salvific task alone. My background provided the language, mythology, and patience to assist a Moses-like business leader in this journey. Besides, I was the only one in the company who had a core competency for dealing with executives who believed themselves to be infallible.

What eventually surfaced was a compelling business need and a messianic CEO pushing forward to meet it. Recruited in the process was a former monk who had some odd skills to offer and divine connections to make. Over time, a relationship formed and grew.

However, that is not how it all originally started. During my first year at the company, I jumped at every opportunity to become competent in the business world and a traditional corporate man. I designed and implemented the company's performance appraisal system and trained all of management in the evaluation process. I was successful and got promoted.

By the second year, I had firmly established myself in a corporate setting and had begun dating a wonderful woman in the company's finance department, a bright accountant with an MBA. Love was blossoming. Life was good. In early spring, a brief visit to the dermatologist revealed a fatal surprise: incurable cancer at its most advanced stage. For the next year I volunteered for an experimental treatment of aggressive chemotherapy and full-body radiation at the National Cancer Institute outside of Washington, D.C.

I survived and came back. I even got married to that lovely accountant. But I was changed. It was bad enough that I had 15 years in the monastery as my sole business training. I now had a near-death experience causing me to see the world from a radically different perspective. The doctors made it clear that I was not "cured." They didn't yet know how patients would fare with the experimental treatment. So even though I felt fine one day, I could be dead the next.

Armed with this information and having a new bride at my side, I gave up climbing the corporate ladder and decided to reposition priorities. I also wondered: If my career is truly over and I could be dead tomorrow, what did I want to do with my limited time? I kept recalling the words of Oliver Wendell Holmes: "Most of us go to our graves with our music still inside us." I began to take his advice to heart.

At work, I decided to spend more of my time being authentic and contributing to the corporate common good. I also spoke my mind, took more risks, and developed a greater sense of humor. One of the advantages of surviving terminal illness is you really don't care about outcomes. At the end of the day, if I was still alive, I considered it a success. The monks refer to this as "holy indifference"—making sure your intentions are pure, then courageously moving forward.

I found myself in a large corporate bureaucracy, no longer concerned with career advancement, more interested in doing the right thing instead of being politically correct, and increasingly focused on coupling my new business skills with my old priestly ones. This is not your traditional recipe for business success, and certainly not behavior that you would expect to capture the eye of the CEO. Much to my surprise, Bob Catell and I came to connect. And when we did, it was just a matter of time before I was called in and told that I was being promoted, relocated to a larger corner office, and given a direct reporting line to the CEO.

"Thank you," I said. "Is it because I'm such a good project manager?"

"Not really," I was told. "The company has lots of directors who can manage projects. And most of them are more efficient at it! But you seem to have other skills. You listen; employees trust you; you have some common sense; you show courage; you don't reposition your opinion when senior management is in the room; and you treat all employees, both union and management, equally. We're hoping you can help the company change and make some progress with employee commitment."

Oddly enough, what corporate America taught me was that the best thing I did for my business career was to forget about having one. It revealed that focusing on unmet corporate needs and trying to be of service could be a workable mix. I also came to see that much of my business work could also be priestly: listening; healing; improving trust; offering faith; asking forgiveness; building community. I naively thought I had to leave my deeper self behind to make it in the world of work. Bob Catell made me see things differently.

Who would have thought that journeys of epic proportion take place not only in the Bible, but also in business? Who could have imagined Moses as a CEO for the twenty-first century, modeling hope and courage in leading employees through the uncertain wilderness of corporate change? How many of us suspected that the economic and the spiritual would be so intimately connected in the human journey?

This book won't tell you how to make your executives more spiritual. They're probably just fine the way they are. Nor will it tell you how to make your workplace more holy. The secular has more than enough of the sacred marbled into it, if we just pay closer attention.

What this book will explore is a serendipitous relationship between two men with radically different backgrounds, yet a similar passion. They join together for the sake of merging money with meaning to make a company different. Not perfect; not world-class. Just refreshingly different.

This book is a chronicle of some interesting stories from the workplace. After all, this is where most of us spend the majority of our time, and it is often the place where we get to use our God-given talents. It is also the locale in which we work out the deeper questions of our life journey: What is our vocation? How do we make a living and not lose our soul in the process? Can our businesses make the world a better place for our children? How might we use corporate and personal wealth to heal the woundedness of the world community? What will be our legacy after we're gone? The workplace also seems to be where the Divine loves to show up: to assist, direct, and have some fun. Mammon and God do mix. This story is just one such instance.

CHAPTER ONE

~

The Funeral

The secret of success in life is for a man to be ready for his opportunity when it comes.

—Benjamin Disraeli

One autumn evening in 1994, on the eve of his company's one hundredth birthday, Bob Catell got up from his desk on the twenty-third floor of the company's gleaming new headquarters in downtown Brooklyn and headed to the elevators. As he punched the button for the second floor, Catell felt a twist of anticipation and trepidation. His destination was the corporate auditorium, where he would help preside over the company's funeral.

Brooklyn Union Gas Company had died, at least symbolically. In his three years as president and CEO, Catell had come to understand that a new era was beginning in the energy industry, and in order to compete, Brooklyn Union had to reinvent itself. It had to wade into the rising tide of deregulation, into new, competitive marketplaces, and find a strategic path to growth and profitability. The old comfort zone that characterized this cozy, monopolistic entity was being torn apart, brick by brick, and a century's worth of business identity, capability, and culture was being confronted with a dramatic challenge: Change quickly or become irrelevant.

In his three years at the helm, Catell had enjoyed the last vestiges of a long period of sustained growth at Brooklyn Union. Starting in the late 1950s, the natural gas business had blossomed into a sweet spot in the energy market, a clean, plentiful alternative to oil, and Brooklyn Union had taken full advantage in selling to its densely populated marketplace. By the early 1990s, it had saturated its existing territories in Brooklyn, Staten Island, and Queens. With more than one million customers, Brooklyn Union Gas owned 80 percent of the residential market and 50 percent of the commercial market. Sure, it owned the pipes in the ground, and as long as the winter winds and frigid temperatures chilled New York, customers would need to heat their homes and offices. But this annuity had no room for growth and expansion. Catell understood an age-old business tenet: Stagnation generally leads to extinction.

And there was more. The New York Public Service Commission, the watchdog government agency that controlled rates and regulated the state's energy industry, had followed the Federal Energy Regulatory Commission's call for deregulation. In the mid-1980s, interstate gas pipelines, heretofore run as tightly protected monopolies, now had to open up their systems to other transporters. Local distribution companies like Brooklyn Union had always been a captive market, forced to buy from the pipeline company that controlled its territory. Now, they would have a choice. Like deregulation efforts in other industries such as airlines and telecommunications, the notion was that an open market would foster competition, reduce prices, increase service quality, and be good for the consumer.

The distribution companies themselves became the next targets. They, too, would have to open up their pipes so that other sellers could offer gas to local customers. Much like the telephone companies in the late 1990s, the energy distributors were being thrown, like it or not, into a new and chaotic business environment. The rules were being changed almost overnight, and in pure Darwinian fashion, those who adapted best would survive.

Catell, in his short tenure as chief executive, had done a reasonable job as steward of the Brooklyn Union legacy. In his 36 years at the company, he had risen up the ranks, admirably impressing his bosses at every stop with his business instincts and his people skills. He was a quick study, and he had that intangible but alluring characteristic that the company's executives couldn't ignore: He simply loved the gas business. He read every periodical, joined every relevant association, attended seminars, and established relationships in every corner of the global gas network, from South America to Calgary, relationships that would give him not only knowledge but access.

In 1991, he was the natural choice to succeed Elwin Larson as CEO, and in early 1994 he'd been handed the chairmanship of Brooklyn Union as well. It should have been—and was in many ways—the perfect endgame of a textbook business career.

But Catell was discontented. He had never been much interested in being a steward and then sliding nicely into retirement with a fat pension and a stately condo in Florida. About 15 minutes after becoming CEO, he had been asked to describe his vision for Brooklyn Union. "I'd like us to become the premier energy company in the Northeast," he had replied.

With tough competitors like Con Edison and Enron, that had been a bold prognostication. But Catell believed that Brooklyn Union had the kind of solid foundation and strong management force to make that vision real. Now, three years later, he was not so sure. He felt a malaise settling in on the company as the realities of deregulation began to seep into the halls and out in the field. Brooklyn Union was in the early stages of a metamorphosis, and people were dragging their feet, procrastinating, even ignoring the new realities. They had grown to love the Brooklyn Union culture, as had their mothers, fathers, and uncles before them. Change might be flying through the air at them, but they would prefer to duck out of the way rather than reach out to grab it.

Catell understood that he was entering the toughest, most daunting era in Brooklyn Union's long history, and as its ninth CEO he didn't want to be the one to drop the ball. Decisions made on his watch would determine not only the company's future success or failure, but whether it would continue to exist as an independent entity at all.

So as he stepped out of the elevator, Catell felt a clear twinge of that business cliché: It is indeed lonely at the top. Kenny Moore, the former monk who had become something of corporate confessor, facilitator, and psychologist rolled into one, awaited Catell outside the conference room. The funeral had been Moore's idea. His reasoning was simple and pious: In order to begin something new, something else must come to an end. One could not embrace the future until the past had been properly and ceremoniously left behind. People held funerals when loved ones died. Why not a similar service when a beloved company passes on?

Though it might have struck most executives as outlandish, Catell was intrigued. He was beginning to believe that *outlandish* was what he needed to shake things up around here. Catell had called on Kenny Moore more often in recent months. In his work setting up corporate performance reviews and a high-level management by objective program, Moore had brought a unique perspective and insight to Brooklyn Union. There he had been, sitting with senior-level executives, helping them set annual goals on which their performance would be measured and their compensation levels set. Yet he had no business background at all.

Feeling terrified and inadequate, Moore nonetheless had plowed ahead and begun to realize that it wasn't business knowledge that mattered. A good deal of his value lay in the very experiences he had left behind in the ministry. When it became clear to those with whom he was consulting that Moore had no personal agenda, no political aspirations, no particular interest in self-aggrandizement, something amazing happened: They opened up to him as they would a priest in a confessional.

He heard their complaints, their anxieties, their biases, their laments. His years in the service of the Divine and his visceral understanding of the human condition gave him a natural filter for their pain. After working for 15 years with the poor and the hopeless, these issues did not daunt him. If anything, he was energized and recognized that he had something invaluable to bring to his job. Corporate

America, it turned out, was a haven for lost souls, and his resume suddenly seemed more relevant than ever.

Moore sensed Catell's anxiety and smiled, offering words of encouragement. He handed Catell a few pages of remarks that the chairman would give to open the proceedings. The gathering had been set up under the auspices of Catell's monthly leadership meetings, regular 90-minute forums in which Catell met with managers and staffers to update them on the company's business issues. The 400 employees waiting inside were chatting and schmoozing, but they all had some sense that this leadership meeting would be unlike previous ones.

As Catell and Moore stepped inside, the room quieted. Catell was still getting used to the effect he had on the corporate population, but he was poised to move ahead. He already knew that there would be plenty of skeptics in the audience that day. He had been mildly skeptical himself when Moore had presented him with the idea, but he had also begun to believe that the path to the future was going to steer well outside the white lines, the comfort zone, of the past three decades. If a funeral could help separate the past and point the way toward the future for his employees, he would gladly deliver the eulogy.

The CEO

~

*H*ow hard was it to effect change in a 100-year-old utility? Well, early in my tenure as CEO, it took three board meetings for me to convince our directors to change the name of the company from Brooklyn Union Gas to Brooklyn Union. Obviously, there was a deep comfort in holding on to the past.

In the early 1990s, I knew we were going to have to become an energy company, not just a gas company. We had to start thinking about new, competitive markets and expanding our products and service offerings. And in order to help the marketplace understand our new mission, I felt we had to change our image, even if it was a subtle change. So I went to the board of directors at our monthly meeting and said, "We're evolving into an energy company, so I think it would be appropriate to change the name from Brooklyn Union Gas to Brooklyn Union." I didn't even suggest Brooklyn Union *Energy*, just Brooklyn Union. There was dead silence in the room. I said, "Okay. Why don't you just think about it for a little bit, and we'll revisit it later."

For our next meeting, I decided to pull out all the stops and do it right. I had my people make up a slick audiovisual presentation of what the new logo might look like, the signage, the trucks, everything. We would get rid of the gas flame in the logo and use a snazzy new modern logo, blue on a white background. I went back to the board and made my presentation. At the end of my talk, one of the directors said, "You mean, you want to take 'gas' out of the name?"

I thought to myself, "You're going to have the shortest CEO tenure on record. You can't even get a simple name change approved." To the board, I said, "Okay, well, why don't you think about it a little bit longer." At the third meeting, I said, "We've talked about the name change at two meetings. I really believe it's the right thing to do, so unless you have any objections, we're going to get it done." No one objected. The name was changed. But it took three board meetings to do it.

That is a graphic example of how traumatic change can be for a company, especially one with a century's worth of tradition. And that was what I was thinking about as Kenny and I entered the company conference room for the "funeral."

I greeted my senior officers who were milling near the door. I was aware of a palpable skepticism about the event. We'd had discussions about it beforehand, and I had heard the objections. "Isn't this kind of foolish? Won't people think this is a hokey thing to do? And worse, could we risk losing a lot of what was good about the old Brooklyn Union?"

I've always been a voracious reader, and I had read enough to know that the most successful leaders tend to heed their gut instincts. I generally seek input from a variety of people—trusted advisers, colleagues, consultants, and friends. I'm a strong believer in building consensus because it not only gets people on board but it provides me with a set of ideas, thoughts, and opinions that I can process to make my call. In the case of the funeral, I decided to follow Kenny's lead. There was something about his approach that intrigued me. He had a way of thinking about things that I had not encountered either inside or outside the company. He could somehow verbalize what I sensed intuitively about the things that people care about, what makes them feel good about themselves, and how they respond to each other and to their managers and executives.

Kenny's insights weren't drawn simply from years in a monastery. In his role in human resources (HR), he was out among the people, from the very senior-level executives to hourly union workers. He wasn't a missionary or prophet. He was simply making up for lost time. He worried constantly about his lack of business training and understanding of the gas business. If he was going to learn quickly, he had to talk to everyone, suck up knowledge like a sponge, and apply his education to his role within human resources. Along the way, he would share with me what he saw and heard— good, bad, and indifferent.

Much of what he does is accomplished by the way he does it. He is thoughtful, provocative, gentle, and good-natured. He presents things in a useful way that promotes positive action rather than anger and retribution. He doesn't say, "Catell, you've got a problem out there. The troops in Greenpoint are going to revolt." Instead, he offers honesty and insight. And that doesn't mean he sugarcoats things or holds back bad news. He has come and told me many things I wasn't happy to hear about, and he has had the courage to tell it like it is. But he doesn't cross the line from a standpoint of trust and confidence.

And in doing all this, he helped me understand the role that I play as a CEO in a corporation like this: how people look at me, watch me, see me, and how I should interpret and respond to their perceptions rather than just my own. He has pushed hard all along the way for me to get out with people and not sit up in an ivory tower, isolated and out of touch.

When we met to talk about this funeral, we were in the early stages of this relationship. We had never talked explicitly about Kenny's background, though I knew he had been in the priesthood before coming to work here. Being a practicing Catholic, I felt that connection resonating within me. It wasn't something I verbalized to Kenny or anyone else. But it was as if Kenny had arrived at the company with a mission, a mission he couldn't visualize when he first started working but one that formulated itself over the years.

In my 36 years at the company, I had never considered a formal integration of the business and spiritual life. There was always a clear separation of church and state, and my religious life, while strong, was outside the office walls. Or so I thought.

I always believed in people, in treating people with respect and dignity, in doing the right thing. For me, this was as natural as breathing. It was a philosophy that I had lived with as a child and that had been stamped deep within my being. It never occurred to me that there was anything spiritual about my working life. You just did what felt right, and more times than not there would be a positive result.

Yet when I became CEO, I started to think about what made our company different from others in our industry as well as in other industries. Sometimes, when you are too close to something you can't really see it clearly. One could argue that more than 30 years with one company certainly made me very close to my surroundings. And it did. But through diligence or cleverness or just pure luck, I had always been able to see and feel Brooklyn Union from a step back, from enough distance to witness the differences, to understand that our people felt just a bit more connected to their jobs and the company than other workers felt about their companies.

I owe that appreciation to the fact that I had worked in nearly every part of the company at one time or another. I'd been out in blizzards in the streets of Brooklyn with crews uncovering broken pipes in the ground. I'd been to disastrous fires where lives had been lost and our crews had worked for days without rest fixing resulting gas leaks. I'd been involved in seeking out new, competitive arenas for the company and traveled around the world to find sources of natural gas to feed our customers' needs. I'd climbed the corporate ladder, but I'd taken time to get off the ladder at each level and wander around, getting a feel for the place.

The conclusion I had reached before I became CEO, and which was strengthened when I took that office, was that we had something indefinable but special, intangible but very real. This company did have a soul, if "soul" is defined as management guru and scholar Charles Handy puts it: "The sense of contained capacity, a sense of going places, of leaving something of themselves behind for others to feed from, of a whole that is greater than its parts, of an essence which infects and inspires. It is the necessary ingredient in great teams and, increasingly, in all organizations." And it was perhaps not just an ingredient but *the* ingredient that triggered the company's long-term success. Needless to say, it was something I wasn't about to take lightly.

These intangible feelings are hard to quantify and even harder to control. It is like the cliché about herding cats—a good idea but difficult to execute. When I entered the room, I had the hope that Kenny's idea would be a major step for me as CEO to reach out and connect with the soul of this company.

The room was darkened and the setting somber. I stepped up to the podium. Behind me, Kenny had set up a mock headstone that read "Brooklyn Union Gas—R.I.P." There were flowers and candles, and as I spoke, Kenny donned his old priestly stole and waited off to the side.

I leaned toward the microphone and looked out at the group. We had all been to many of my monthly leadership meetings before, but there had been nothing like this. This meeting was all-inclusive. Employees from all levels of management as well as from the union bargaining units had been invited. Many had been invited because they were known to be key influencers within the company, people who would take the message back out to their colleagues and spread the word. The faces looking back at me were expectant and alert. What, they must have been thinking, is he going to say about all this?

"Good evening and welcome," I said somberly. "For almost 100 years, we have been a gas utility serving Brooklyn, Queens, and Staten Island, regulated by the Public Service Commission and restricted from certain lines of business by government mandate.

"With the arrival of deregulation, all this is changing. Our business model is moving away from a traditional utility company and toward that of an energy company, a company that is no longer functioning as a monopoly but will be competing with other energy providers for a growing share of the marketplace.

"Where we used to be a monopoly, we will now face competition. Where we used to be guaranteed a reasonable profit, we will now be vulnerable to greater swings in our revenues. Where we used to be severely restricted on the lines of business into which we could venture, we will now have greater freedom to compete.

"The coming of deregulation will be very new to many of us who have spent our entire careers in this company. While some of what will be happening will be unsettling, much of it will be exciting. Where there are some vulnerabilities here for us, there are many more opportunities for our business and our industry. But all this will demand change for us. While some utilities may be caught off guard by these changes, we will not. I am excited and optimistic about these new opportunities for all of us.

"But it's helpful to remind ourselves that change is less a singular event and more a journey. And Kenny Moore's program today will give us a sense of how we can embark on this journey and what we might find along the way: the losses, the gains, the hopes and possibilities.

"In order to begin the journey, we must consider that some of the changes we are going to experience have their origins not with a beginning but with an ending. There will be some sorrow and loss that we all will feel in abandoning our old ways of doing business, as well as when we take up the new skills required to successfully compete in a deregulated environment. In the process, we will experience an in-between time—when the old rules no longer apply and the new rules have yet to be defined. This will make many of us feel anxious and unsure.

"However, this in-between time, this transition period, while ambiguous and unsettling, is necessary before any progress can be made. We are required to first mourn the loss of the known and spend time wandering around feeling lost and alone, the way we would feel if we lost a loved one. Only then are we ready for a true beginning.

"There are many examples of companies that have tried to change, yet failed, largely because they didn't understand that employees' first reaction to any change is to experience a loss. This ending of the old, with its requisite confusion, anger, and depression, needs to be acknowledged and incorporated into any corporate change effort.

"I need your continued support and passion to bring this company into this new era. We need to remember that we are not abandoning everything that is dear to us. Quite the contrary. We have created something very unique and special over the past century at Brooklyn

Union and we intend to retain that uniqueness as we move into the future. We are a company that cares about its people, its customers, its stakeholders. That is not just talk; it is evident in the actions of our people every day, every week, every month, every year.

"Today is a time to honor and recollect what we were, a memorial to an era that is now concluding, an act of remembering, embracing, mourning, and moving on. And perhaps most important, it is an occasion to affirm that you are not going forward alone. We are in this together and we share all the anxieties and fears of the unknown. We may grieve individually, but we will move forward collectively and I am confident that the best is out there ahead of us."

I stopped speaking for a moment before turning things over to Kenny. There was a long pause, that moment when it isn't clear if applause is warranted. I was glad for that moment because I really wanted this to have time to sink in, for people to know this wasn't some program du jour. By being here and putting my stamp of approval on the event, I was hoping to send a strong message.

The funeral, in the long run, had a strong impact. I admit that I was surprised at how effective it actually was. People still remember it, nearly 10 years later, as a turning point for the company. It spawned a company-wide initiative that we called Back to the Future in which, over the course of 18 months, we brought all the employees together, both management and union workers, for daylong meetings and workshops. Meeting in the morning with senior officers, the employees were asked to think about their past and their place in the company as well as the present and the future. In afternoon breakout sessions, they were encouraged to voice their fears, concerns, and feelings about where the company was heading. It provided a forum that the funeral had begun and a chance for employees to get comfortable with the coming changes.

The funeral was a turning point for Kenny and me. It cemented our relationship and gave me confidence that these kinds of efforts were well worth trying, no matter how nontraditional or off-the-wall. I began to believe that Kenny had something special in his ability to see ways to move the company forward. And I was smart enough to start to use that ability more and more.

The Monk

~

As a man steeped in religious traditions, I know something about funerals. When I was a priest in the monastery I presided over many of them. All had taken place in the confines of a church and involved bestowing divine blessing upon the faithfully departed.

This one would be a bit different. It was held in a corporate auditorium, memorializing the demise of an old way of doing business. While some questioned the value of hosting a company funeral, to me it seemed like the natural thing to do. Rituals and ceremonies are part of the human experience and predate organized religion by thousands of years. You didn't need to be a monk to pull it off, but it probably couldn't hurt.

When life comes to an end, whether personal or corporate, we naturally want to mourn that loss, acknowledge our grief, and seek support from those around us. All this is healthy, for it heals the soul and helps us move forward productively. If I was able to assist my former parishioners with this task, I figured I was competent enough to do it for my present ones as well. Some habits die hard. In many regards, it was the same skill with just a different venue.

After Bob's introduction, I solemnly stepped to the podium dressed in my dark blue suit, the corporate equivalent of a Roman collar. For dramatic effect, I placed my priestly stole around my neck and switched on a tape of Gregorian chants to properly set the mood. I thought of burning some incense as well, but feared setting off the smoke alarm.

"Dearly beloved," I intoned. "We are gathered here today to bid farewell to our company's past. This century-old tradition has served us well; but alas, we must pay our respects and say good-bye." I looked around the audience and saw confused as well as bemused faces. Many employees wondered whether our life as a monopoly had truly come to an end. Senior management saw the writing on the wall, but many of the employees didn't. They wondered, why embark upon a change if everything seems to be going well? Death sometimes has a way of sneaking up on you like that. One day you're fine and feeling comfortable. The next day, rigor mortis sets in.

"Bob was right when he said things are changing," I continued, "and it starts not with a beginning but with an ending. Our former way of conducting business is dead, and attending a funeral is one timeless way of acknowledging that loss. As a company, if we can't say good-bye to the past, we won't be able to embrace the present. And we'll miss out on the future."

Having never hosted a *corporate* funeral before, I felt a bit ill at ease. But I was no worse off than the 400 employees before me who had never attended one either. "We embark upon this ceremony with a sense of reverence for all that has come before us. We must lay it to rest with dignity and respect."

Employees' reluctance to see the consequences of deregulation was the compelling reason I had used in convincing Bob to host this funeral in the first place. "Until we start publicly confronting their denial, we're not going to transform the culture," I had told him. Our workers would continue doing business as usual, believing that nothing had really changed. From a corporate perspective, we needed to make our executive business conversations more public. Only then could we hope to effect dramatic change. Involving large numbers of employees in these discussions creates momentum. Ultimately, workers will support only what they help create. So bringing them together to include them in the conversation is powerful. I had been able to convince Bob of this. I was hoping that today's ritual might be enough to sway the skeptical crowd before me as well.

"Grieving friends, it would be most appropriate at this time of our mourning to identify those things that are over for us as we bury our beloved past. I invite you to solemnly share with me those qualities, behaviors, and business practices that must be buried—here and now—for us to successfully move into deregulation."

On a table near the back of the stage, I had placed a small funeral urn and some blank index cards. I was ready to move into action. "What I'd like to do is write down on the cards some things that have ended for us as a company." More empty stares from the crowd. "So, group. What's over for us as a business?"

After what seemed like an eternity, one accountant spoke up: "You mean, like the loss of job security?" "Exactly," I said and wrote it on the card and dropped it reverently into the funeral urn. "What else?" Slowly these reluctant mourners got into the swing of things, calling out other aspects of the business that were quickly becoming a thing of the past: guaranteed profits; lifetime employment; secure growth. One embittered supervisor even said that the future career of the "white male" was likewise a thing of the past. I wrote it all down and placed it in the urn without comment.

"Let us now pause for a prayerful moment of respectful silence for what has gone before us." I scanned the auditorium and saw a sea of smiling faces, smirking yet engaged. Taking some "holy" water, I blessed the urn and explained that while our past needed to be interred with respect, deregulation was inviting us into an unknown future. Out of the corner of my eye, I noticed Bob smiling. I hoped he was feeling a bit more comfortable that he had opted to support this event.

As I turned off the Gregorian chants, the crowd grew silent. "Funerals not only acknowledge an ending, they also prepare us to move forward." To represent the next phase of our corporate journey, the in-between time, I rolled onto the stage a replica of the *Santa Maria* from the art department's Columbus Day display.

The boat signified the feeling of being disconnected, out there between ports, in this corporate transition. I reminded everyone that we could expect to feel very much like explorers on the high seas: nervous, scared, and insecure. Pulling a deflated life vest from beneath the podium, I grabbed a young engineer from the front row and placed it around his neck. "In uncharted waters, we'll need to find ways to stay afloat. What might we as a company need to do to keep buoyant during our transition, as the business rules get rewritten?"

The audience began to get engaged in this drama of our corporate journey. They shouted out their answers. "Teamwork," declared one employee, quickly followed by "Better use of technology." I wrote them on the cards and now pasted them on the life vest to "inflate" it. The group got the idea. "Listening to customers can't be overlooked," offered a third. Soon the vest was covered with the future needs of the company.

We were now ready to move to the third and final part of our drama-journey: the new beginning. Since we didn't yet know how deregulation was going to affect us, I wanted to use this last segment as a chance to do some visioning work. Pushing the *Santa Maria* aside, I brought out a large replica of a stork with a newborn babe in tow, borrowed from the company's Valentine's Day display. Sure, it was cheesy, but I had no budget for props.

"Even though our journey started with an ending, it inevitably brings us back to a beginning. Similar to the birth of a baby, there is still much uncertainty about how this new life will all play out." I wanted to spend some time focusing on the future. Directing them to blank posters on the walls, I invited them to use their artistic skills and draw pictures of what they wanted Brooklyn Union's future to look like.

"Use images and symbols to represent your thoughts." Now eager to participate, people flocked to the posters and drew. Some executives even joined in with crude art and ready suggestions. One group drew a battle scene, with victorious employees taking the field. Another drew dollar bills floating down from the heavens with union workers getting their fair share of corporate profits. As I observed all this from the stage, Bob took the opportunity to walk around the auditorium to offer encouragement. We spent a few minutes hearing employees explain what their artistic renderings meant and then brought the meeting to a close.

"Similar to the birth of a baby, your drawings reflect our collective hope for Brooklyn Union's future," I concluded. "While there's no guarantee that all this will transpire, it demonstrates our collective commitment to making it happen." I raised my hand in final benediction and turned the meeting back to Bob, who gave his closing comments and invited the group for refreshments in an adjacent conference room.

As I left the auditorium, the chief financial officer pulled me aside: "I have two things to say to you," he said. "One: You have some set of balls! And two: I'm not sure anyone else but you could have pulled this off." I took it as a compliment, of sorts.

Bob was pleased with the funeral. It was unorthodox, but it had sparked the kind of discussion we would need to move forward. It was indeed just a beginning.

Three years earlier, when I first started working with him, the focus was on helping his leadership team embrace change. Working on the executive floor was a bit different than working in a monastery. When I was behind the cloistered walls 50 percent of the people thought they were divinely inspirited. In business, the number was up to 80 percent. Nonetheless, my job was to help these executives develop business goals to drive the company into the future. They were tied to an incentive compensation plan. Meet the goals and there was a payout; miss the mark and money would be lost.

In sitting with the senior officers to set their goals, I regularly witnessed discussions of Bob's performance. Often their remarks focused on his shortcomings. Much of what was said I chalked up to corporate sibling rivalry and petty carping. Yet a few of their gripes seemed to strike at the heart of effective leadership. "He wants our opinions, but spends little time listening to our replies," someone said. Another moaned: "If he doesn't agree with your alternate plan, there's no room for discussion." Several lamented: "He sometimes gets preachy; when that happens the group turns him off." I realized that I had been a bit naive to think that sermonizing affected only the clergy.

Believing that Bob would benefit from hearing these comments, I brought it up at our next update meeting. "What I'm about to say falls into a 'take it for what it's worth' category. I'd recommend that you take no immediate action. Simply listen. If anything strikes you as worthwhile, do with it what you want.

"Your executive team thinks that some of the things you do get in the way." He looked quizzical. I summarized their frustrations and continued on. "You ask a lot of questions, but don't have time to listen to the answers. Some see you as aggressive when dealing with those you disagree with."

"Aggressive? How so?" he asked me.

"I've been told that if you can add the words 'You jerk!' to the end of a sentence, you're being aggressive. Sometimes your staff experiences you that way." I spoke of other traits that I felt compromised his management style, all with the religious compassion that my spiritual guides of old had used on me.

"Anything else on your mind?" Bob inquired.

I was already in deep, so I continued. I knew that many employees remained ignorant of the challenges facing the company as well as Bob's plan of response. There was a need to get him out of his executive office, to spend more time among the workers. The way I saw it, Bob's business agenda had many of the same characteristics as organized religion. If he wanted to change the company and get employees to believe, he'd be required to spend more time with them. The early church fathers used to say that religion is caught, not taught. To garnish employee passion and commitment, direct contact with the "faithful" would be required.

In medieval times, the followers of Saint Francis of Assisi wanted to know what to do when they took to the streets. "Tell everybody about the love of God," Saint Francis advised. "If necessary, use words." The business world calls this "walking the talk." But for me, it had its origin several centuries ago. I believed Bob would be well served by following Saint Francis' advice.

"You have thousands of employees out there who need to be directly tied to your vision. Focusing executives on the right goals is only part of the solution." I knew that there were many cynics who required conversion in order for this venture to succeed.

"Consider yourself like Moses. You're freeing the people from a perilous past and trying to bring them to a future promised land. And that probably will include some time wandering around in the desert." When Moses led the Jews out of Egypt, he walked with them, talked to them, and listened to them. "It seems to me that's the kind of thing you should be doing if you want to move the company into the future."

Aware of Bob's silence during my monologue, I looked up. He remained quiet for a while. A long while. I wondered if I had overstepped my bounds. "You know, Kenny," he finally said, "there's some truth to what you say. I'm not opposed to changing some of my behaviors. Unlike you, I don't spend a lot of time examining my conscience. So maybe it's a good idea for you to keep me informed. But don't expect me to always be a model penitent. I still have a business to run and a corporate culture to change." I was surprised at his candor.

"And while I'm no Moses, I get your point about the need to stay in touch with the ordinary workers. Sometimes I feel removed from their day-to-day experiences and need to reconnect. I'm also concerned that some negative things are being kept from me. You know, the fear employees have in being the bearer of bad news. Maybe you can also help me here?" Obviously, I wasn't shy about sharing bad news.

"I might be inclined to help," I told him, but I was also concerned. "I don't want to position myself as a spy. As you know, some people speak to me almost under the seal of confession and I'm not interested in violating those confidences. But I do see a lot—both good and bad—and I'd be willing to share my counsel with you."

I offered my services as his intermediary. I also offered him my candor and directness. "Please understand, whatever I say is more my perception than any dogmatic truth. The last time I looked, only God had cornered the market on that." But I believed that we were sitting on a world of great possibilities, with employees who were talented and committed. If we could tap into the wealth of their passion, I felt the company's future would be brighter. "I'm willing to work with you on this."

Bob was pleased. "I like your unique perspectives and refreshing insights," he said. "Besides, I get the feeling that people trust you and your opinions. It might be worthwhile for us to continue these 'take it for what it's worth' conversations on a regular basis."

He asked that I schedule regular meetings to keep these conversations going. A part of me was wondering what exactly I had gotten myself into. As I got up to leave, I offered him one final bit of advice: "Just a reminder, Bob. It took Moses 40 years to lead the Jews to the promised land. I don't think you have that much time. You'd better start praying now."

At dinner that night, my wife Cyndi asked: "So, how did your day go?" "Just fine," I said, feeling pretty good about the course of events. "I had a chance to meet with Bob and tell him about some of his management flaws. I also shared with him how he's contributing to the problems on the executive floor and what's ticking off some of the employees. All in all, I thought the meeting went well."

With the insight of a seasoned businesswoman and the affection of a beloved spouse, she warmly replied: "You said *what*? To *whom*? Are you crazy? You don't do things like that in business! Need I remind you that we have bills to pay and a big mortgage hanging over our heads? Please stop experimenting with stupid ideas—you'll get yourself fired. Just keep your mouth shut and do what they tell you."

I tried to interpret her comments favorably. But it was difficult. My 15 years of celibacy had not adequately prepared me for the wrath of a woman with an MBA in finance.

In some regards, business is a lot like the Church. Change creates unmet needs, and those who can address them have a greater chance of getting their talents used. In institutions undergoing change, when unfounded rumors fly furiously, there is a select market niche for someone who can be trusted by all sides to help sift the wheat from the chaff. A person who has the corporate common good at heart and is not disposed to sell his soul for monetary gains could be a useful catalyst. This was a niche I was willing to fill.

Thus began this unique relationship between Bob and myself, which has lasted for over a decade. It was an odd union—a hard-driving CEO and a slightly damaged but enthusiastic former monk. It was not a marriage made in heaven, but rather one forged in the marketplace. It was not a typical business relationship. But it was salutary.

CHAPTER TWO

～

Brooklyn Union, the Fertile Hen

Of all the properties which belong to honorable men, not one is so highly prized as that of character.

—Henry Clay

Bob Catell understood better than anyone the implications of his daunting new job. This was not a Silicon Valley start-up or a Wall Street financial institution, with little history or communal loyalty. Brooklyn Union was, in many ways, more than a company. It was an institution woven into the very fabric of its surroundings. Letting go of the past was no easy task when the past was as long and dynamic as Brooklyn Union's.

Relatively few corporate entities exist for more than a century. Fewer still remain situated in and connected to a single community the way that Brooklyn Union had been throughout its history. Its roots, like its vast network of gas pipes, lay deep within the streets of Brooklyn, Staten Island, and Queens. The company routinely hired from within its own geography. The people who worked there lived in the neighborhoods and were also customers. Rare was the employee who did not have a relative—a father, mother, uncle, aunt, brother or sister—who also worked at the company.

And working at Brooklyn Union was a distinction, a cause for admiration and even envy. You didn't go there to get rich. BUG people, as they were known, didn't drive Cadillacs or wear fur coats. But a job at Brooklyn Union meant security, a roof over your head, food on the table for your kids. And it was a job for life. The company never had layoffs, and few left. The attrition rate, in fact, has always been minuscule compared to those of other companies and other industries.

The goodwill engendered by the company throughout its service area was palpable and real. Unlike other utilities, when a Brooklyn Union meter reader or repairman rang the doorbell, he or she was greeted with a smile. Housewives brought out cakes and lemonade for Brooklyn Union crews digging up streets to repair gas mains. These weren't anonymous workmen disrupting traffic; these were neighbors, friends, and relatives working for a good company that took care of its own.

The company's heritage was rich and colorful, despite its status as a regulated utility. Its birth and swift growth were the product of the dramatic transformation of Brooklyn itself. Brooklyn, the independent city, became a borough of New York City in 1898. With new bridges, trolley lines, elevated railroads, and even new subways helping to urbanize Brooklyn, its population exploded as the twentieth century began, growing from 1.2 million in 1900 to 1.6 million in 1910 and to more than 2 million by 1920.

In the late nineteenth century, as Irish, Italian, and eastern European immigrants along with Swedes, Norwegians, Danes, and Finns crowded into the borough's many distinct neighborhoods, the business possibilities associated with such growth became obvious to the opportunistic capitalists who founded the company. More people meant more light, more heat, more gas.

Not surprisingly, the movers and shakers who founded the company had close ties to John D. Rockefeller's ubiquitous Standard Oil. This kind of gas, called "water gas," was manufactured in giant coke ovens as a by-product of coal. It was used primarily for illumination. At the turn of the century, another form of gas used for heat, called "fuel gas," was also becoming popular. With the widespread use of electricity for lighting still years away, the gas business began to surge.

In the battle for control in this burgeoning metropolis, financial giants like Henry Huddleston Rogers and William Rockefeller, John D.'s younger brother, were instrumental in consolidating the seven independent gas companies operating in Brooklyn into Brooklyn Union Gas Company. The new company was officially incorporated on September 9, 1895.

Ironically, in 1884, Rogers and Rockefeller had also been instrumental in founding Consolidated Gas Company, which eventually became Consolidated Edison, one of the nation's largest energy companies. They could only have dreamed that one day these two companies would become the two biggest energy companies in New York City.

Rogers was so renowned in his day that upon his death in 1909, he merited a page 1 obituary in the *New York Times*. The financier was a charming, shrewd, and sometimes ruthless businessman. Among his closest friends was famed author Mark Twain. He personally rescued the writer, enmeshed in a string of bad investments, from financial ruin. Twain, under his real name Samuel Clemens, became one of the first and most enthusiastic stockholders in Brooklyn Union.

Twain closely tracked his investment in Brooklyn Union and called it "a fertile hen. Let her lay as long as she can." When Rogers died, the writer was among his pallbearers at the funeral. "I owe more to Henry Rogers than to any other man I have known," Mark Twain wrote. "He is not only the best friend I have ever had but is the best man I have known."

The company grew quickly as demand for its products rose with the fortunes of the boroughs it served. Fast growth continued in the 1920s, spurred by a new wave of migration, this time African-Americans moving up from the South as well as out of Harlem. Puerto Ricans seeking a new life away from their island country also began to arrive by the thousands.

The Great Depression hit Brooklyn as hard as anywhere else, maybe more so, but decisions made during that treacherous time only served to solidify Brooklyn Union's reputation. In 1935, facing drastic declines in revenues, then CEO Clifford Paige dropped the company's rates voluntarily in an attempt to help strapped customers afford their energy needs. "A Utility Lowers Its Rates" trumpeted an editorial in the *Brooklyn Eagle*. "It is a bold step and one which cannot but reflect favorably on the management of the company, regardless of the outcome," the newspaper wrote approvingly.

Paige's largesse was an early example of the "enlightened self-interest" that came to characterize Brooklyn Union. Such a move was considered revolutionary at the time, but the net result justified the step. Sales indeed surged throughout the remainder of the 1930s and into the 1940s. Profits may have been scarce, but the goodwill was priceless.

Paige set the tone for Brooklyn Union CEOs to come. He was a hands-on leader at a time when such ideas were anathema to business. He routinely handled customer problems himself and personally called on the families of employees and retirees who had died. He became one of Brooklyn's most visible civic leaders during his tenure.

And as the country emerged from World War II, Brooklyn Union was poised for a period of strong and sustained prosperity. Ironically, the 1950s began a period of decline for Brooklyn itself. As the decade progressed, Brooklyn-based industrial corporations began to move away to cheaper suburban locations or other cities. White, middle-class residents also began to flee, lured by the green lawns and white picket fences of growing suburban areas in Queens, Staten Island, Long Island, and New Jersey. In 1957, the harshest blow of all came when the beloved Brooklyn Dodgers decided to relocate to Los Angeles, with its exploding population, abundant land, and ceaseless sunshine. Broken hearts have never healed.

Over the next few decades, Brooklyn was staggered. This once proud U.S. manufacturing center saw its manufacturing output fall by one-half between 1954 and 1990. Its waterfront fell into disuse, and even the famed Brooklyn Navy Yard closed. Neighborhoods sporting row upon row of elegant brownstones fell into decay and poverty as the 1970s saw rioting, arson, and surging crime rates displacing people and neighborhoods.

Yet Brooklyn Union prospered, in no small part because it remained committed and active within a changing community. The pipes were in the ground. The company wasn't going anywhere except to expand its own horizons into new, alluring territories like Staten Island and Queens, where it planted stakes in the ground just as these suburbs began to pulse with growing new populations.

But the great makeover of Brooklyn Union, the catalyst for Brooklyn Union's emergence as a twentieth-century energy powerhouse, was the company-wide conversion to natural gas in the early 1950s. Under CEO Hugh Cuthrell and his protégé John Heyke, the company abandoned the costly, inefficient, and increasingly scarce manufactured gas that had fueled its success from the beginning. The future, they rightly believed, was in the abundant and potent natural gas.

The conversion from manufactured to natural gas was a massive undertaking at Brooklyn Union. In just six months in 1952, the company converted 950,000 homes, stores, factories, and plants. More than 2,300 miles of pipeline had to be emptied and refilled, and more than 2 million appliances such as ovens and water heaters were adjusted without a single mishap. With one stroke, the company's coke ovens were closed forever and Brooklyn Union became a very different company.

When Cuthrell died in 1953, Heyke became the company's youngest CEO at age 43. He was a visionary leader who understood the dynamics of his marketplace. He foresaw the changing Brooklyn and took measures to expand the company's horizons; at the same time he remained committed to his home base. If the customer base was unlimited, a utility had to do little more than keep signing up new accounts and switching on the gas. But if the territories, even while expanding, were ultimately finite, a company had to change its focus from a utility to a marketing-driven organization.

Heyke recognized that there was a vast market out there waiting to be conquered. Converting oil customers to natural gas was going to require sales and marketing. In that vein, Heyke made salespeople into stars in the new Brooklyn Union. In the 1960s, he courted desirable customers like real estate mogul Fred Trump, a New York developer and Donald's father. He convinced Trump, who was building new properties at a frenetic pace, to install natural gas in all his buildings.

Under Heyke, the company unveiled a pioneering, computer-based customer service system built on a $2 million IBM mainframe computer. Customers could now call in to a single location and a service representative could have their account appear in seconds on a computer terminal. This unprecedented capability offered faster service, less confusion, and the sense that Brooklyn Union was connected tightly to its customers.

But in his 21 years at Brooklyn Union's helm, Heyke did more than prime the business pumps. He raised Paige's concept of enlightened self-interest to the level of a corporate asset. Doing good not only was the right thing to do, but it paid off. If Brooklyn Union got out in the community, made a commitment, and sent its employees to volunteer for countless neighborhood organizations, committees, and charities, the community would respond. When rate hikes became necessary, the outcry that other utilities faced was muted or silent when it came to Brooklyn Union.

In 1966, Heyke decided to do something about the degeneration of Brooklyn's neighborhoods. He sent his people out to find a decaying, uninhabited building and instructed them to refurbish it from basement to attic.

A four-story 1883 Victorian, situated at 211 Berkeley Place in a blighted part of the Park Slope section of Brooklyn was purchased for $15,000 and renovated with care. It became a showplace for visitors, and the media took notice. The company dubbed it the Cinderella Project and promptly began purchasing more homes set for renovation. Combing the most deteriorated neighborhoods like Bedford-Stuyvesant, it found more renovation projects and in short order had converted dozens of downtrodden homes into desirable residences. The houses were resold at a minimal profit, and the intangible payoff raised the concept of enlightened self-interest to a new level.

The response to Cinderella was overwhelming. The media swarmed to the story and the company was hailed by community leaders, politicians, customers, and regulators for its foresight. Brooklyn Union's visibility reached new heights. Fred Rider, a company vice president who drove the project, said at the time, "It made people realize that we meant business. And our reputation went through the roof."

When Heyke died unexpectedly in 1974, an era came to an end. But the company had a tradition of grooming talented successors, and its success had attracted a growing cadre of smart and aggressive young executives. Eugene Luntey, followed by Elwin Larson, steered the company through a turbulent period of growth and controversy, marked by natural gas shortages, a painful 13-week work stoppage, and the onset of deregulation in the energy industry.

Entering the final decade of the millennium, Brooklyn Union had managed to pull off something akin to a business miracle: As it approached its centennial celebration, it had sustained profitable growth, it had emerged as the leading gas distribution company in the Northeast, and through all that it had retained its sense of spirituality and compassion. As massive change loomed ahead on the horizon, its soul was intact.

And it had another asset. As the new decade began, Bob Catell became president and chief operating officer. A year later, he became chief executive officer. The first Brooklyn-born CEO since James H. Jourdan, who had been Brooklyn Union's first leader a century earlier, Catell was part of a new wave of corporate officers who had grown up in Brooklyn and at Brooklyn Union. For Catell, Brooklyn Union had been far more than a job. His entire life was inextricably intertwined with this company, and in his heart he knew he was in exactly the right place at exactly the right time.

The CEO

~

I think it's fair to say that Brooklyn is in my soul, deep and everlasting. Almost all my childhood memories come from the avenues, the schoolyards, and the parks of Brooklyn. I remember the celebrations in the streets on V-J Day at the end of World War II and the shoeshine box I took to the Ninth Avenue subway station to earn some money when I was 10 years old.

I was born in 1937 in the Borough Park section of Brooklyn. I lived in the same fourth-floor walk-up on 43rd Street for the first 24 years of my life, and certainly the person I became was formed from the experiences of that neighborhood and that life.

My father took me to a ball game between the New York Giants and Cincinnati Reds at the Polo Grounds when I was about seven years old. It is one of my last memories of my father. He and my mother divorced when I was eight years old, and he died soon after. I've never talked much about him since then. He was Italian-American, and my family name was originally Cicatelli. When he started working, he decided to Americanize the name by lopping off the first and last letters and shortening it to Catell. He was Catholic. My mother was Jewish and her family came from Russia.

We certainly were not what you would call a very religious family. Because of my parents' diverse backgrounds, we celebrated both Catholic and Jewish holidays. I was bar mitzvahed in the Jewish tradition but we also had a Christmas tree. My first wife was a practicing Catholic, and when we had a family I became one as well, which I remain to this day. That said, I've never been especially religious, at least not in the strict, organized sense of the word.

Growing up without a father, with the war coming to an end, in the vibrant, pulsing Brooklyn of the 1940s, I truly didn't have time to dwell on religion. My mother taught me and my younger sister that nothing in life comes easy; you have to work hard for whatever it is you are going to get. I believed that if I got an opportunity and made the most of it and it was recognized, that good things would happen and I would progress. I never shied away from a job. I worked hard at it even if I didn't particularly like it.

I was a good student, not a great student. I managed to earn an undergraduate degree from the City College of New York and then, after a two-year stint in the army, went back and got my master's degree in engineering. I got hired as a junior engineer at AT&T but quickly realized that I was one of about 200,000 employees and in a company that big, my opportunities to advance would be slim.

Brooklyn Union, a small gas company in Brooklyn, was hiring. It was June 1958. I went to the headquarters building on Remsen Street and landed a job working in the meter repair shop in the Canarsie plant. Even in those days of *The Man in the Gray Flannel Suit*, I could never have dreamed that this would be the only place I'd work for the rest of my career. But I've been with Brooklyn Union, now KeySpan, ever since.

And my career at KeySpan has been, in many ways, like an unending series of graduate school courses in business and management. Every position I've held, and I've been in many, has been an incredible learning experience that set the stage for the next opportunity. I certainly never dreamed that I'd end up as CEO. My starting salary was $450 a month, and I remember my goal back then was to earn $10,000 per year. If I ever got that much, I thought, I'd have made it. I was happy to get a good performance review, a small raise, and a promotion. But at each stop, I soaked up everything I could—the people, the issues, the strategies, the competition, the customers, the political environment—and how it all mixed together to form the realities of a job.

It is impossible to recount all the indelible moments of a 45-year career, so I won't even try. What stand out, however, are a few experiences that were milestones on my rise to the top of the organization, experiences that not only shaped my own career, but infused in me the values of the company.

At the meter repair shop, for example, I was just a kid out of college thrust into what turned out to be a tension-filled situation between the union and management. In those days, meter mechanics got paid for the number of meters they repaired in a day. The more they repaired, the bigger the paycheck. It seems archaic today, but that's how it had been for many years.

Management decided it was time to change the operation from the piecework model into a production line. They brought in a consultant to help design the new organization and sent an assistant manager to oversee the reorganization. I assisted him. My job was to walk around the plant with a clipboard and capture statistics on the mechanics' productivity. You can only imagine how popular I was down there—a 21-year-old, wide-eyed kid keeping tabs on these grizzled union veterans.

I was truly terrified. This was a hot, noisy shop filled with sweaty, burly union men working with soldering irons. I was walking around in a suit and tie, taking notes and asking questions, and people were not too happy. I had an uneasy feeling that one day I'd feel a hot soldering iron stuck between my shoulder blades.

I found myself in the middle of this very difficult and tense situation. The union didn't want to change because they felt their members would lose an opportunity to supplement their wages if a new system was installed. Their representative was a brawny bargaining unit guy named Peter Derwin. He was tough but very smart. On the other side was the general shop foreman, a sturdy, street-smart Scotsman named Angus McNorton.

As green as I was, I somehow befriended both of these men and became an intermediary between management and the union. I got to know the workers as well and they got to like me. I made it clear to them that I wasn't a spy and had no axes to grind. I was accepted and felt that I contributed in some small way to tempering a difficult situation. Most important, I learned from both Derwin and McNorton about the union and its relationship to management. I came away with a deep respect for the union leadership and the difficulty of their position. I gathered insights in how to deal with the unions and how to present management's position in a meaningful way. Mostly, they taught me lessons about how to work with different kinds of people in stressful situations, and these were lessons I've never forgotten.

In those days, Brooklyn Union was simply a microcosm of the city. The workforce was a melting pot—Italians, Irish, Jews, African-Americans, Polish, Greeks. It called to mind Moss Hart's words about New York in his autobiography, *Act One*: "The only credential the city asked was the boldness to dream. For those who did, it unlocked its gates and its treasures, not caring who they were or where they came from."

Everybody was related to somebody. I don't think I met anyone who didn't have a relative in the company somewhere. And the exuberance that followed the war held steady throughout the 1950s, happy days mostly, or at least that's how most people remember them. I felt that energy as I came to work every day.

Thus began a series of moves within the corporate hierarchy, moves that took me out into field operations and later into various management positions in engineering, distribution, gas operations, customer service, and sales. In 1961, when I began what was my only stint as a hands-on engineer, the union workers went on strike for six long weeks, seeking higher wages and better benefits. What I learned from this experience couldn't be taught in a classroom.

Suddenly, as part of management, I found myself out on an emergency truck in the field. There I was using a jackhammer, breaking pavement, digging holes. We had to cross picket lines and work in 12-hour shifts in order to stay on top of the work. It was exhausting and sobering. It hit directly at the company's core values and gave me a firsthand view of how tenuous the relationship between management and labor can be. Valuing people, listening to what someone has to say, and trying to stand in the other person's shoes are all critical ingredients to making the relationship work on a lasting basis.

In 1971, I was promoted to assistant vice president. I didn't see myself on a fast track at the time, but it was clear that I was well thought of by senior management and was being given a tremendous amount of opportunity to experience every piece of the company's business.

It should have been a glorious time of great promise and excitement, but my life at work was being impacted by events at home in my personal life. I was beset by difficult personal problems as my marriage began to come apart. I came to the conclusion that it might be better for me to leave Brooklyn Union and start a new career elsewhere. I looked around and searched out some new opportunities, even briefly considering going to work for the gas company in Hawaii. But Gene Luntey, the CEO, and El Larson, who was executive vice president at the time, took me aside and gave me counsel.

Gene said to me, "Bob, we care about the job you are doing, and we care about you. You need to deal with your personal problems, but if you just continue to do a good job for the company, things will work out for you."

What struck me was that here was the top guy in the company taking a personal interest in my life. We were not a huge corporation at the time, probably under 4,000 employees. But still, here was the CEO taking this young middle manager under his wing, addressing a very personal crisis in a sensitive, caring way. And this was not an isolated example. This is how things were done at Brooklyn Union, and it made a lasting impression on me and reinforced my feelings about how you deal with people. In those days, well before the New Age concept of companies as family, this company really *was* a family. If a family member got into trouble or had a problem, you stood by them. Brooklyn Union had an impeccable reputation as a place where people liked to work. It was a leader in its industry and did right by its customers and employees.

I handled my personal problems and realized that I had made a smart decision to stay where I was.

And if the company was making an impression on me, I was making an impression on the company. I was clearly on a leadership track, and what I did and the way I did it seemed to be getting noticed. When I was a field engineer in the distribution department, for example, I often worked with outside contractors. Inevitably, a city contractor offered me a bribe, a financial reward to be treated "differently" in his words. I turned him down, told my supervisor, and was never tempted by a quick financial reward. Others saw this as integrity and honesty. I wasn't naive. I knew what went on in the streets and outside the meeting rooms and other corporate settings. But that wasn't my style or the company's, and in Brooklyn Union, that attitude served me well.

All during this period, I was heavily involved in the American Gas Association and other industry-related organizations. I felt I was being shaped not only by this succession of jobs but by the people I was meeting along the way. I realized that I'd been blessed with the ability to relate to and work with all kinds of people, and that is, in my opinion, at the heart of what leadership is all about.

By the mid-1980s, Gene Luntey retired and El Larson became CEO. I was promoted to executive vice president and chief operating officer, and it was clear by then that I was being groomed to eventually move into the CEO suite. Somehow, I had played the game correctly simply by not playing the game.

Brooklyn Union was not exempt from politics. People jockeyed for position just like at other companies. But I never aspired to a specific job and refused to play the political games associated with executive musical chairs. I decided early on that if you work hard and do a good job, you'll get recognized. I'm sure that's naive in many organizations, but it worked in my favor at Brooklyn Union. I've never once asked for a raise or a promotion. I achieved a reputation for getting things done well and quickly, two characteristics that will never hurt you if you are angling for a better job. And to be honest, by somehow eschewing the desire for a specific position, getting it was all the more sweet.

Entering the 1990s, as I became CEO, Brooklyn Union was poised to become a very different company. Not only the name, but the very essence of the company itself, would have to change over the course of a turbulent and frenetic decade.

I remember praying for guidance, for the strength to do the job.

No one is ever completely prepared for the emotional and psychological impact of being handed the top job in an organization. I had a sense that despite all the skills I had acquired along the way that had prepared me intellectually for this position, there was going to be something else that would play a significant role. A search for the soul of our company was not something that entered my mind, but in many ways that's what I was embarking upon.

I didn't really know Kenny very well back then. But serendipity has always been my companion throughout my personal and professional life. And the eventual realization that I wanted and needed a deeper, spiritual connection to this company was going to require many things to come together at the right time, luck included. In some ways, I was beginning the last leg of a journey that had begun decades earlier in the streets of Brooklyn. I wanted it to be memorable. I had no idea just how memorable it would be.

The Monk

≈

I grew up ordinary, the third of six children, in a two-bedroom row house in Flushing, Queens. In many regards I was uncommonly curious. In my youth, this trait worked against me. I was a lot like the prizefighter Rocky Graziano, who was forced out of school in the sixth grade because of pneumonia—not because he had it, but because he couldn't spell it. My school record bore the scars of one who was unwilling to swallow pat answers and regurgitate them back on command.

My curiosity had me asking too many questions, holding too many opinions, challenging too many authorities. I didn't always see things the same way as my teachers, something the nuns at St. Luke's grammar school didn't take kindly to. As one who grew up on the streets of New York, I also brought a sense of mischief to my dealings with those in authority. Although school didn't reward me for these many "gifts," life eventually would.

Throughout my youth, I was an altar boy at St. Mel's parish. In contrast to the scandal of priestly pedophilia that mars the Church's name today, I experienced our parish priests' affection as chaste and caring. Their warm benevolence had a favorable impact. Even at an early age, I was left wondering if God might likewise be calling me to follow Him in this special way. This attraction would stay with me as I continued to grow.

My father's death from heart disease at age 48 left me with a few profound lessons: Life was precious, and reaching old age would not be guaranteed. It also strengthened my resolve to live my life to its fullest—something that would serve me well in my later adult years as I came to battle cancer and bounce back from my own heart attack.

My dismal academic record made it difficult for me to gain acceptance into a seminary, but I persisted. Finally, I received an acceptance notice . . . of sorts. It was a tentative note from a strict religious
order, the Salesians of St. John Bosco. I could come and live in their
religious community and start a program of study. If I could adjust to
the monastic lifestyle and complete the college course material, we
could continue the conversation about becoming a priest. The
monastery was nestled in the rolling hills of Sussex County, New Jersey, a terrain largely populated by cows and dairy farmers. Once
there, I found the religious lifestyle to be austere. I felt woefully inadequate and realized that I had much catching up to do. Yet with hard
work, it was happening.

I made my vocational choice in an era of hope and renewal for
Catholicism. Making mistakes would be inevitable, and as the monks
would come to so graciously teach me, God didn't really care much
about our faults, anyway. The Almighty was far more interested in our
efforts and willingness to respond. And through some special grace, I
found myself willing to respond to a vowed life of poverty, chastity,
and obedience.

The religious life I lived was populated with men of humor and
wit. There were also many with a staunch moral mandate that strove
for societal change and religious action. They were fiery souls, full of
passion and commitment. The Salesian order dedicated itself to serving the needs of the poor and abandoned.

One quiet monk, who grew up destitute in the ghettos of South
America, understood firsthand the intractable nature of poverty.
Early one morning in chapel, Brother Jacob gave a bold sermon
based on the Brazilian proverb: "When shit becomes valuable, the
poor will be born without assholes." I was at first somewhat taken
aback that monks would use that kind of language. But then I was
reminded of Jesus' words to the Pharisees: It's not what comes in or
goes out of a person's mouth that makes him holy, but rather what
resides in the depths of his heart. So here was a monk with a foul
mouth, but a holy heart. And I would come to meet many more
characters like this on my journey. It's one of those apparent contra-

dictions that for me further revealed the Divine's sense of humor and irreverence.

While some members of the community didn't approve of Jacob's colorful choice of words, he felt it accurately reflected the plight of the poor. When chastised by Father Superior for the foulness of his language, he responded with humble arrogance: "Go lodge your complaint with the thousands who will die today of starvation." He was more interested in being true to the poor people he ministered to than to the social niceties of religious decorum. Even though he was reprimanded for his visceral views, he was never ousted for them. Brother Jacob modeled the monastic belief that whoever is not angry when there is cause for anger sins. His years in the ghetto taught him to take a stand when one needed to be taken. For me, Jacob's presence served as a living reminder that the interior life required not only that we pray for the poor, but that we also incur obligations to take public action to remedy perennial injustices.

The monks seemed to resonate with what the American Catholic writer Flannery O'Connor once wrote: "Most of us come to the church by a means the church does not allow." The church was very forgiving and accepting of the foibles of the human journey. This odd mixture of sanctity, social reform, and idiosyncratic behaviors would eventually become part and parcel of my religious tradition, one steeped in responding to the needs of a modern world, yet with a slightly twisted sense of humor. Oddly enough, the playful bantering with authority that I learned growing up in the streets of New York got recast into something the Catholic tradition warmly referred to as "holy disobedience." You shouldn't always do what you are told. There are higher laws than compliance and rote responses. I came to learn that those who speak definitively and with moral certitude about the mysteries of the sacred are to be held suspect. Time and again the rigors of the interior life invited me not to be individually perfect but to be an instrument in service of a perfect God. It didn't matter that I stumbled or fell. There were sacraments and grace readily available to anyone who asked.

We rose before dawn, scurrying around in monastic silence to get ready for morning prayer, meditation, and Mass. We all wore black cassocks that warmed us in the cold of winter and exhausted us in summer's heat. With the completion of the evening's final prayer service, the monastic community was enveloped in something called "The Grand Silence." No words were spoken; monks retired to their rooms for personal prayer, reflection, and graceful sleep. No communication would take place until breakfast the following day.

Death was a big thing for monks. My religious order had a spiritual practice called "The Exercise for a Happy Death." Though it sounds morbid, it was rather refreshing. On the last day of each month, you spent an entire day alone reflecting on death. It was a chance to see what you were doing right and wrong. It was a time to leave behind the distractions of the monastic day-to-day world, go inside yourself and get clear on what is important. There would be prayer services and a chance to confess your sins to the priest. Some would spend the time planning their own funerals.

After 12 years of study and apostolic work, I was ordained a priest. The spirituality I came to discover in the sacred confines of the cloistered life was refreshing and attractive. Like Don Quixote of old, I was following the impossible dream, and it became a daily way of life. But after 15 years of following that dream, I realized that for me it was indeed impossible.

My years in monastic life were a wonderful and sacred journey, yet ultimately unsustainable. I came to see that it lacked personal intimacy. As recent priestly scandals have revealed, some of my peers were seeking destructive ways to compensate. While I had not experienced any sexual abuse in my monastic journey, I was no longer feeling I could authentically live my life in the cloistered confines. Even though my soul flourished, my human spirit floundered. Like the thousands of celibate priests who left their ministry to return to the secular world, I, too, walked away from my religious vocation.

I don't believe that most of us take our vows or make commitments with the intent of breaking them. But we do. Sometimes for the right reason. Other times, not. I returned to the world, still curious, and looking to find a more sustainable expression of my desire to collaborate with the Divine.

In leaving the confinement of religious life, I suddenly found myself in the confinement of my widowed mother's home. The transition back to the world was as challenging as the one that initially took me away. It was both slow and humorous. I remember walking down to the local bank and being interviewed for my credit card application. The questions came fast and furious: Credit history? "None," I sheepishly replied. Bank account? "None." Present income? "None." Place of employment? "None." Residence? "I live down the block with my mother." The bank officer looked at me like I had just landed from outer space. That was pretty close to how I was feeling, too.

Even though I had mastered the arcane medieval rituals of monastic life, I was ill prepared for the rules of dating and initiating a job search. My sisters encouraged me to visit some of the singles bars and try to meet other people. I quickly came to learn that 15 years in the monastery was not a good preparation for the New York City nightlife. Being financially poor, living with your mother, and having no job or car didn't make the process easy. In the post-Woodstock era of free love and sexual liberation, it wasn't all that clear to me that being an adult male with his virginity still intact was an attractive quality.

Searching for a job was just as surprising. I remember going on an interview at Chase Manhattan Bank, which ended with the employment manager telling me: "Mr. Moore, you're obviously a very talented person. But we don't have any jobs for *talented people*. We're really looking for someone with accounting experience. I'll give you a call if anything turns up." I waited for the call. It never came.

Religion and money have a long and intertwined history. I knew in my heart that I wasn't as ill prepared to get a job as some imagined. It would take me awhile, but I slowly learned how to translate the skills of the monastery into the language of the world of work. It was through my ever-growing list of networking contacts that I came to Brooklyn Union Gas.

Fred McPhilliamy, the executive in charge of the human resources area at Brooklyn Union, was both an astute businessman and a devout Catholic. Even though I had no corporate experience, he felt that I had marketable skills. "If you were able to handle the politics of the Catholic Church, you'll have no problem in corporate America," he said. "It's pretty much the same stuff."

Once hired, I was impressed with what I saw at the company. This 100-year-old enterprise had many of the same characteristics as the 2,000-year-old institution I had just left behind. Not that any of the employees were particularly "religious," yet these people had a clear sense of purpose and passion. They seemed to sincerely care for their customers, their service territory, one another. I was meeting ordinary people who demonstrated some extraordinary characteristics. They were sincere, hardworking, decent people who brought a sense of family to the world of work. They regularly engaged in magnanimous activities, which executives said were based on sound business principles, but seemed to me to be more akin to charity. Although I was miles away from my monastic environment, I was feeling oddly at home.

After two years, I was promoted within the corporate ranks. I also met a beautiful young co-worker named Cyndi Presto and embarked upon my first significant romance. We had just finished celebrating my 38th birthday with a picnic lunch in Central Park and a romantic dinner together when I stopped by the dermatologist's office to get some medication for a minor skin rash. In the course of the examination, the doctor said: "I notice that you have enlarged lymph nodes. Is that normal for you?" "What are lymph nodes?" was my fateful reply. "Get it checked out," he said. "It could be something serious." I did. It was.

My yearlong bout with cancer drastically altered my life. I eventually returned to work, but I had been changed. Despite my illness, Cyndi and I had gotten married. Climbing the corporate ladder and garnering the next promotion were no longer at the top of my list. They weren't even *on* my list. I was newly married and acutely aware that I could be dead tomorrow. When five o'clock rolled around, rather than stay late and impress my boss, I went home for dinner with my wife. If I could be dead tomorrow—which was now a distinct possibility—I thought I'd like to spend my time with Cyndi. With divine good fortune, I survived. We would eventually go on to have two wonderful boys—Christopher and Matthew—who have both increased our joy and compromised our sanity.

As I returned to work full-time after my treatment, my strength returned but I found myself pondering a deeper business question. If my fast-track career was over and I could be dead tomorrow, what did I want to do with my limited time? Meeting Bob Catell would give me a way to answer this question.

CHAPTER THREE

Enlightened Self-Interest

You don't have to sell your soul to make your numbers.

—Tom Chappell

A company with more than a century of history doesn't become spiritually enlightened simply because a former monk doffs his robes and gets a job in the human resources department. KeySpan's sense of values as an organization was created bit by bit, year by year, with the touch of many people, both executives and staff alike, over its long history. Bob Catell and Kenny Moore both understood that their relationship and their mission existed because of, not despite, KeySpan's culture.

Trying to explain such a culture is like trying to re-create a recipe from Julia Child. One can list all the ingredients and provide all the proper instructions but still not create the soufflé quite the way she intended it. The ingredients that make up the KeySpan culture—honoring diversity, integrity, and trust; promoting volunteerism and community service; respecting employees at every level of the company; integrating customer satisfaction as a measure of performance; making philanthropy a business-level commitment—are integral pieces of the company mix. And while many companies preach similar values, KeySpan works to execute on them.

At KeySpan, there has always been an added sense of grace and dignity, born during the Brooklyn Union days, carried forward by one corporate generation after another, and taken to a new level under Catell. It is a hugging culture, a "thank you" culture, a culture where the edges are sandpapered away so that the mean-spiritedness of corporate politics is mostly absent and ideas, even bad ones, are given a hearing and shown respect.

It is Catell, standing for hours in New York's Bowery on a cold Christmas morning handing out some of the 5,000 overcoats collected by employees for the destitute and homeless. It is Moore, who is also a poet and painter, convincing scores of employees to paint and draw and selling their work in the company lobby with all funds going to an inner city charity. It is the 5,662 pints of blood donated by KeySpan employees in 2002, enough to make KeySpan one of the top five companies in the nation in terms of blood donations. It is the company-sponsored gathering on Long Island of breast cancer survivors and relatives of victims, tears flowing down their faces, pinning photographs of lost loved ones on a giant spruce on the front lawn of KeySpan's Hicksville headquarters building.

It is the raucous laughter emanating from conference rooms where Moore, a proponent of humor and fun, has convened yet another offbeat management meeting, bringing in improvisational comedians, artists, and other nontraditional thinkers to explore the trials and tribulations of corporate change. It is Catell, slipping off his jacket on a hot Brooklyn summer afternoon, picking up a stickball bat and slugging a spaldeen down the street during a KeySpan-sponsored community event.

And it is the belief and resolve on the part of the CEO, a man with a laser focus on profits and shareholder value, that a former monk brings such a unique spirit and connection to the employees that he sends him out, unimpeded and empowered, to expose and nourish the corporate soul.

This uncommon attitude about the business and the company's key constituents evolved, much as Catell's relationship with Moore evolved over time. For example, Catell and Moore never discussed

Moore's religious background or monastic experiences. Their first connection came as a result of a program Catell instituted in the late 1980s when he was still executive vice president and chief operating officer of Brooklyn Union. Catell wanted to set up a "management by objective" program for the company's executives. A consultant from Hay & Associates was brought in to create the program and get it up and running.

All executives would be required to develop short-term, long-term, and stretch goals for themselves and their departments. If they delivered, they would make money. If not, their budgets would suffer until they made progress toward the goals. In a company like Brooklyn Union, a regulated monopoly, the idea of accountability, risk, and reward in a highly competitive marketplace was mostly a foreign concept. But Catell knew that deregulation was going to change the nature of the game, and he wanted his top people to be fully prepared for what was coming.

Once the consultant got things moving, Catell decided it was unnecessary to pay the steep consulting fees to run the program. He looked within the HR organization and tapped Moore to take over. For some in HR, Moore's background was suspect as qualification for this new role. He not only lacked an MBA, he had no business background at all. Further, he'd recently returned to the company after a long, life-threatening bout with non-Hodgkin's lymphoma. By all accounts, he should have died long ago. He had returned to work, against all odds, but he was fragile. Would he be capable of taking on such an arduous task?

But Catell turned aside the objections. There was something about Kenny Moore that struck a chord within him. Though he didn't know him well, he sensed that Moore would actually be the perfect person to work with the executives. Moore had the interpersonal skills of a priest, the serenity of a monk, the unbiased attitude of a business neophyte, and a stark absence of a personal agenda. Having cheated death by what Moore perceived as God's abundant sense of humor, he had decided that life was literally too short to become ensnared in a climb up any corporate ladder. He had survived the experimental cancer treatment, but his doctors had made no long-term promises. If each day might be his last, Moore sensibly reasoned, why waste it on corporate politics and infighting?

Catell met with Moore to outline his objectives. Moore listened with great trepidation. He felt inadequate, ignorant, and unqualified for the position. He would be sitting with the chief financial officer or the chief engineer, and he had no background in their disciplines. How could he purport to help them set objectives? It would take him years to get the business acumen to offer such insight.

Fearful as he was, Moore was spirited forward by Catell's confidence in him. And what he quickly realized was that he didn't need the business background to accomplish the task. The CFO knew what was needed to set financial goals, as did the chief engineer regarding project design and development. What they needed was someone to help them shape and define their objectives and put them in the perspective of the people and the organization.

As it turned out, they needed something else as well: an outlet to vent their frustrations and anxieties and concerns about their roles and their place within the organization. Moore inevitably began to hear complaints about Larson (the CEO) and Catell. These were not personal attacks because both Larson and Catell were well liked. Instead, they were criticisms of decisions, strategies, communication skills, and the usual detritus of corporate territorialism. Moore understood that most of the executives were alpha males who had their own designs on the top spot in the company and their own ideas about how things should be done. They had dominating personalities and strong opinions, and they were politically astute.

More important, many of their concerns and gripes had validity and were not simply personal agendas. Moore was surprised but pleased with how these executives opened up to him. The meetings took on a small taste of confession, and Moore knew well how to listen to human sorrow and suffering, no matter what the subject or form of delivery. Here, he couldn't grant absolution. But he could become a trusted listener and a wise sounding board.

On his own, Moore found other avenues to understanding. He regularly visited and talked with people lower in the corporate ranks—department heads, managers, administrative assistants, union workers. He'd quiz them on how they viewed a situation that had been presented in a certain way by a senior vice president. He would often hear a very different take on the same issue, usually offered with the insight and understanding that one can get only from people who are out on the front lines of the business.

As a result, he was able to report back to Catell in a way that was wholly unexpected; not always pleasant, but ultimately useful and welcome. When he delivered his updates to Catell, they were not presented as espionage but instead as enlightenment.

Considering he was talking with the chosen successor to the CEO, Moore was notably unabashed. He made a point at each session to explain Catell's contribution to the problem as well. Speaking frankly to Catell seemed less imposing after his long stretch in the Church and certainly after his close brush with death. When one works for the Divine, he reasoned, a president or CEO just wasn't that monumental. He saw himself as akin to Hebrew National hot dogs: He reported to a higher authority.

Moore admits that his personal outlook created "bravery." But he also understood from his days in a religious order that authenticity is a value; working toward the common good is a value; holding people responsible and accountable and contributing to their success is a value. And clearly this is what Catell gleaned from the conversations.

Later in their relationship, after Catell became CEO, Moore suggested that Catell spend more time out in the field with all levels of employees. One idea that Catell quickly embraced was the "Break Bread Dinner." Moore invites six employees, usually midlevel managers or directors, to join Catell at a restaurant for dinner. The setting is informal, the ground rules simple: just feel free to talk and ask questions and spend some meaningful time with the CEO.

Catell, an inveterate people person, loves the concept. The employees, usually nervous at the outset, warm up with a glass of wine and the realization that Catell has no hidden agenda and is remarkably approachable despite his lofty title. Moore generally sits quietly, occasionally facilitating, mostly listening and observing.

After one recent dinner, he sent Catell his assessment:

> Again, the feedback after you left was very favorable. The chance to meet informally and in such a small group continues to impress. And that you listened and invited their comments was very well received. I liked the new tone of your questions and would recommend that you continue to initiate this conversation. Much is changing and some of it is not pretty—it's worth asking them their feelings about it, how other employees are responding. Continue to be sensitive about speaking too much, asking them more open-ended questions, and being quiet in the face of their initial silence. This will reveal very beneficial information. . . . As you know, most employees would be more than willing to spend the entire dinner listening to you speak, but that gets us very little. Don't let them off the hook even though it feels a bit unnerving to deal with the awkward silence.

Rather than being defensive, Catell welcomes Moore's candor. It took some getting used to at the outset, but Catell quickly saw the vast potential of this new link to his company. Some messages surprised him, some confirmed his own suspicions, and others he was already well aware of. He receives them mostly with humor and grace, and when he gets angry, he declines to shoot the messenger. He realized when he first began his work with Moore that he had established a relationship that would serve him well when he became chief executive.

And on the other side, rather than seeing Moore as some Machiavellian schemer with the prince's ear, the executives and employees welcomed this distinctive intermediary into the mix. They had never had an informal but effective spokesperson, someone without a personal agenda who could present their views at the highest level. Moore's presence was scrutinized and deemed acceptable, even desirable. Moore listened. He had the quiet, introspective, and comforting presence of a man of the cloth. If people had been skeptical early on, they came to see Moore as a consistent source of insight—in some ways, a consultant who never left. People in companies tend to scrutinize the new and unusual. At KeySpan, they saw the small, private moments that defined Kenny's kindness, patience, and thoughtfulness. As Henry Hoffman said, "Character is what you do when nobody is looking." The word around the watercooler was, "Kenny is okay and can be trusted."

Moore began to read business literature, educating himself with Tom Peters, Michael Hammer, Peter Senge, and Stephen Covey. He would send *Harvard Business Review* articles to Catell after underlining passages that had relevance to the company. Often, Catell would route those articles to his executive team.

Catell's initial brush with Moore has grown into a significant reliance. In the late 1990s, he formalized the relationship and named Moore "corporate ombudsman." He sent a memo to all employees: "Many successful companies have an employee on staff who is accountable to the CEO and is viewed as a trust figure by employees," Catell wrote. He noted that Moore would remain a neutral, confidential, and independent resource for employees. "The role of the ombudsman is to serve as an embodiment of the corporate conscience and will have three features: confidentiality, impartiality, and the corporate common good."

It was the embrace of the corporate common good that framed the relationship between the two men. For those who had grown up at Brooklyn Union, the odd couple, the CEO and the monk, felt somehow familiar, comfortable. The very notion of a corporate conscience, an oxymoron within most companies, seemed natural and appropriate. For newcomers, it presented a strange but enticing tableau.

Elaine Weinstein arrived at Brooklyn Union in the mid-1990s after 11 years at Merrill Lynch. Having spent nine years as a social worker early in her career, Weinstein had become a training and organizational development executive at Merrill Lynch before joining Brooklyn Union. As senior vice president of human resources, she has closely observed Moore's work within KeySpan and is a vocal supporter. In fact, she often refers employees to Moore and seeks his counsel on difficult HR issues.

She notes that ex-nuns and ex-priests are not uncommon in corporate settings. But most make a significant transition. They go to graduate school, earn business degrees, and become accountants or marketers or designers. Few, however, carry their former personas into corporate roles as Moore has done—coaching, mentoring, teaching, serving as a confidant. Given recent corporate history, it would be a stretch to imagine such an influential player with a similar mandate at companies like Enron, Global Crossing, and WorldCom or the airlines, investment banks, and brokerage houses.

"This says more about the company than it does about Kenny," Weinstein says. "And one of the reasons I came here was that when I met the senior team, I found them to be extremely bright, as smart as anyone running a Fortune 500 company. But there was something more, a level of compassion, a level of commitment to employees and a kind of instinct about people which is very important to them.

"It's not about religion," says Weinstein. "It's about, as Kenny puts it, 'getting the hearts and minds of employees to create a motivated, empowered workforce that is committed to the company, because we embrace that kind of difference.' It's actually very simple."

For Weinstein, KeySpan represents a matchless confluence of characteristics. As a native Brooklynite, she grew up witnessing Brooklyn Union's influence on her neighborhood and community. She was familiar from childhood with what she calls "the magnanimous nature of the company, its true charitable giving in terms of dollars and time." The reputation stemmed from the very real commitment that was and remains a core value of the company mission. In 1995, then New York City mayor Rudolph Giuliani called Brooklyn Union "the best corporate citizen in the city of New York."

When Weinstein joined the company, she noted that a core of its executives—like Catell; Wally Parker, president of KeySpan Energy Delivery; Bob Fani, president and chief operating officer; Lenore Puleo, executive vice president of client services; and others—had been at the company for all or most of their careers. This experience of growing up together and moving into leadership positions together spawned a family feeling, a mutual respect even with the usual disagreements and turf battles that flare in any business organization. As a utility, there is a blue-collar sensibility, a humble quality that is embodied not only by Catell but also by much of the workforce, management and union alike.

"There's a very warm feeling, a camaraderie that's very strong," Weinstein says. "It may take a while for new people to be accepted here, but once they are, they're embraced. It doesn't mean it can't be tough. They expect a lot from you. They challenge you and come down on you when you are really screwing up. But even then, it's about the work, not you as a human being."

It is not surprising that the attrition rate has been preternaturally low, barely 1.5 percent when most companies are at 10 percent or more. "It's a little bit higher than natural death," Weinstein says. "People have historically come here for lifetime careers."

Of course, such familiarity is more likely to exist in a relatively small company like Brooklyn Union before it launched into significant growth with a series of mergers and acquisitions in the late 1990s. With under 3,000 employees—and just 800 in management—the culture was easily spread to all corners of the organization.

But whatever the size, the company exuded what Weinstein calls "emotional intelligence," an intuitive social awareness, a valuing of people, a commitment to the community. She points out that the support and concern Moore was given when he struggled through his bout with cancer was not unique. Along with a generous benefits plan, there is tremendous flexibility built into the system that is focused solely on meeting an employee's needs. "It is about taking care of the employees and making sure they are there for their families, for themselves, for their own healing," Weinstein says. "Because what you get then is this enormously committed employee who is very grateful. It's not about guilt; it's just how you build loyalty in a company."

And though she understands its heritage from past corporate generations, Weinstein credits Catell for driving the vision to new heights. "I'm a late starter here and I've worked in big corporate settings, so I can compare," she says. "And while other companies commit far more dollars, no one commits more passion and time than Catell does personally, and asks his executives to do as well. And we do—because we want to."

KeySpan executives are aware of the powerful nature of such cultural commitment and fight to not only keep it in place but spread it out into an expanding organization. Such a rollout of values-laden ideals that emanate from a small, historic core is never easy, especially in the recent bad economy. In most companies, there would be an urge to relegate such behavior to the background and hunker down. Wally Parker, who has been with KeySpan for 32 years, sees it differently.

"I would vehemently argue that tough economic times underscore the need for this type of thing even more," Parker states. "Any good company knows that its only truly sustainable competitive advantage is its people. Goods and services can be copied, but people cannot be. So when you go through tough times, you need your workforce to be ready for battle. You want them fit, mentally engaged, and focused.

"We need to provide the support for our folks, whether that resource is training, venting, stress release, whatever. If we're going through a period where there's going to be more stress and strain, any opportunity for people to develop a better comfort level, to feel free to express themselves, or to find avenues that help them to bond together better, that's all critically important."

The commitment manifests itself through the repetition of a certain behavior that quietly but powerfully impacts those who touch the company. On a Sunday evening, Parker, one of the company's most senior officers, attended a wake for a KeySpan employee, a young woman who had tragically died from breast cancer. She was a union worker, not a corporate officer, but at KeySpan caring has no hierarchy. At the wake Parker spoke to her brother, who was profoundly moved by the company's response. "I'm just overwhelmed by the outpouring of love and concern and caring by your company," the brother said. "The scores of people who came, the flowers. I can't tell you what it means to our family."

Though such commitment to these integral values can be time-consuming, costly, and logistically difficult, the payoff is tangible, both inside and outside the company. Lenore Puleo, a 28-year KeySpan veteran, often works with outside consultants and over the years has received consistent feedback about the company's strong reputation for integrity and honesty. Having spent her whole professional career inside KeySpan, she admits to having little basis for comparison, but the response from outsiders is not only flattering but beneficial to the company's business dealings.

Recently Puleo and a consultant agreed that the consultant's company would be paid a percentage of the savings it helped KeySpan realize from the assignment. There would be no risk to KeySpan and the consultant would rely on KeySpan employees to track and report the savings to him. According to Puleo, "We shook hands on the deal and he said to me, 'If this was any other company, I would never do this. But I trust you and I trust the people at KeySpan. With any other company, I'd need a legal document hundreds of pages thick to outline the agreement. We have a one-page agreement and a handshake. I trust you will be fair and live up to your word.' I thought it was one of the greatest compliments that the company ever got. He was working not just with me but with people from many parts of the company, so it was truly reflective of the company's reputation."

In an era of corporate greed and malfeasance, particularly in the energy industry, the goodwill that KeySpan engenders is a priceless asset. KeySpan executives attribute it to a commitment to ethical behavior, doing the right thing, and finding the proper balance for meeting the needs of its key constituents: employees, customers, and shareholders.

"Trying to do the right thing doesn't mean we are pushovers," Puleo points out. "And we are not perfect by any stretch of the imagination. We admit that, know that, and it's a good thing because we recognize that all this can be very fleeting. You get measured by it every day."

As a utility, with a significant percentage of its revenues coming from highly regulated businesses, KeySpan's reputation for integrity is particularly crucial in the regulatory and political arena. Catell has spent an inordinate amount of time in Albany, courting and impressing key political allies and regulators. Steve Zelkowitz, president of KeySpan's Energy Assets and Supply Group, says that the company's relationship with the state's Public Service Commission is built on an unusual level of conviction.

In 1998, for example, in the earliest days of the politically charged atmosphere of deregulation, the company discovered that an overzealous executive had engaged in unethical conduct in dealing with an unregulated subsidiary that the company had formed in 1996. Because deregulation was new and being heavily scrutinized by the Public Service Commission, such a violation of the code of conduct was likely to bring the Commission's wrath down on Brooklyn Union.

The vice president, a dedicated 20-year employee, had knowingly violated the rules and was quickly asked to resign. At an ensuing executive meeting, Zelkowitz urged Catell to go straight to Albany and admit the violation to the Public Service Commission. While some executives in the room looked at him as if he was crazy, Catell agreed immediately and quickly set up a meeting with the Commission.

"We went up there and it was probably the most difficult meeting I've ever been in at the Public Service Commission," Zelkowitz recalls. "We laid it all out, and after some discussion, they fined us. The fine was in the form of paying for advertising promoting the benefits of deregulation. It was a slap on the wrist and certainly not the worst of all possible outcomes. The chairman of the Commission looked at Bob and said, 'The fact that you came up here personally, were open and honest and turned yourself in, that was very much appreciated and that's why it came out as it did. Not every CEO would have done that.' "

Given that this happened in the midst of a burgeoning economy, where the seeds of corporate shenanigans at giants like Enron were being planted, Catell's hat-in-hand confession had a profound impact.

"They trust us," Zelkowitz says. "We're not secretive. We like to open the books and say, 'Here's what's going on.' In this way, we have a good dialogue with them, and when we have a disagreement with them, it's always respectful. And the result is that they never try to kill us because they know if we're wrong, we'll admit we're wrong and make it right."

Such self-regulating behavior is at the core of what KeySpan calls "enlightened self-interest," the simple notion that doing good for a company's core constituencies will have a positive impact on the bottom line. In a 2002 *Harvard Business Review* article, Roger L. Martin wrote, "The most significant impediment to the growth of corporate virtue is a dearth of vision among business leaders. Opportunities abound to devise programs and processes that benefit society as they enrich shareholders. What seems lacking is imagination and intrinsic motivation on the part of corporations and executives."

This has never been the case at KeySpan or Brooklyn Union. In fact, the company under Catell considers such behavior part of the corporate DNA. In 1996, for example, at Catell's urging, Brooklyn Union initiated its On Track program for customers in New York State.

The program was designed to help customers who cannot pay their bills. Rather than setting collection agencies on people who simply don't have the means to pay, the company decided to help customers change behavior and learn how to care for themselves financially. In fact, Brooklyn Union had always handled delinquent customers in an unusual manner, a practice that continues at KeySpan today. Twenty service representatives act solely as customer advocates, providing information and referrals to customers by telephone, offering aid in finding ways to pay their bills rather than simply shutting off the gas. The On Track program emanated from this. Administered by four staff social workers, On Track helps customers with their immediate needs such as working out a payment plan for the gas or electric bill.

Sending out social workers rather than bill collectors for delinquent customers was novel enough to attract the *New York Times*, which in 1999 published a lengthy feature on the program:

Two years ago, Joy Chatel appeared in Civil Court in Brooklyn to account for her $7,000 unpaid gas bill. A contractor had bilked her out of $40,000, she told the judge, forcing her to close her beauty parlor. She had no income and four grandchildren to raise. When her husband died about this same time, she had to barter two years of free hairstyling for a proper funeral.

The judge instructed the lawyers from Brooklyn Union Gas Company to work out a payment plan with Ms. Chatel, and the lawyers handed her account to Kristen Yontz. Ms. Yontz, though, is not a bill collector. She is a social worker, part of the utility's experiment in getting people to pay their bills by helping them straighten out their lives.

She has met regularly with Ms. Chatel, advising her on low-interest loans, enrolling her in a support group for grandparents, steering her to Federal emergency heating funds, and significantly for Brooklyn Union, placing her on a flexible repayment plan. Ms. Chatel is still struggling, but she has reopened her beauty parlor and soon plans to rent the top two floors of her building.

Offering aid instead of threats has reduced client arrears by an average of 27 percent. But the program goes well beyond that. With the help of professional scriptwriters and producers, the company created a course in money management that is offered via audiotapes delivered for free, along with a tape player and reading material, to the customer's home.

The course is divided into seven episodes written in cliff-hanger fashion like a soap opera. The customer gets an education kit, including file folders, tape recorder, calculator, and all the material they need to learn how to manage their financial situations, not just to pay the gas bills but for all their needs. Along with all this, the company assesses their heating equipment and replaces it for free if need be. Customers also get up to $400 off the amount they owe when they meet the course requirements and start paying on a timely basis.

The program has already paid for itself in terms of outstanding bills collected. Of the original 1,500 customers in the program,

1,100 were paying more than they had before the program began. And several other utilities have emulated the program in their own service territories.

And such enlightened self-interest not only defines KeySpan to its communities but it reflects Catell back to his employees and stakeholders. An organization is a shadow of its leader, and Catell, as Lenore Puleo points, "casts a very big shadow."

All this raises an obvious question: Can this kind of behavior happen while a company prospers? As in most cases relating to business, the numbers don't lie. Under Catell, KeySpan's journey has been a productive and profitable one. Revenues have grown from under $1 billion in 1990 to $6 billion in 2003, while net income has soared from $56 million to $378 million. Company assets were $1.5 billion when Catell became CEO. Today, assets stand at nearly $13 billion. The stock price has risen 80 percent and the dividend 40 percent since Catell took over and the total return to shareholders over that time is 11 percent, higher than the overall S&P 500 Index and more than double the S&P Utilities Index. KeySpan is now the largest gas company in the Northeast and the largest electric-generating company in New York State.

A company indeed can make the numbers, or even blow the numbers out of the water, and very much hold onto its soul. Even in the most difficult economy, as the past three years have demonstrated to KeySpan, the grasp of corporate values becomes more important than ever.

Thus, Moore has flourished inside KeySpan, and those who work closely with Catell understand his relationship to Moore and why it works for this company. "Bob has a rare quality," Weinstein says. "He is someone who is very connected, very compassionate, and believes deeply in his employees. All of us, after 40, 50, 60 years, become prisoners of our own styles, our own history, and our values. And so many of his qualities are lovely; they are qualities you'd like to see in your children, in your partner, and in yourself. So it's not a bad prison to be locked into."

The CEO

~

Sometimes the opportunity for enlightened self-interest arises in unexpected places. In the early spring of 2002, David Manning, KeySpan's senior vice president of corporate affairs, drove me out toward the eastern end of Long Island to a remote and unspoiled stretch of land in a town called Jamesport. In a borrowed SUV, we drove off the road onto a long, empty, and pristine beach on Long Island Sound. It was a cool but sunny day, the china blue sky filled with majestic white clouds. The surrounding vegetation was just turning from brown to green, and the first blooms of spring were evident in the underbrush along the sand.

We walked for a long way along the beach and then made our way up to the crest of a 200-foot-high sand dune overlooking the shoreline. I felt the wind against my face and listened to the water birds flying overhead. As someone who loves being near the water, I was exhilarated.

I've been to many places around the world, but this truly was one of the most exquisite landscapes I had ever seen. The view was simply breathtaking. Standing on the dunes, we could see the Connecticut shoreline. There was a natural, spring-fed lake teeming with waterfowl. There were stands of trees and a web of potential nature trails. I could visualize how it would look in the full bloom of summer. For a guy who grew up on the streets of Brooklyn, it seemed impossible that something so magnificent could be so close to home. I thought to myself, "I grew up in a city surrounded by concrete. There should be spaces like this for our children and grandchildren."

What was more amazing was that KeySpan owned this splendid property. We had obtained it as part of our merger with the Long Island Lighting Company, known as LILCO, in 1998. And after several years of trying to decide what we should do with the 550 acres that we owned here, the answer became obvious to me.

In late October 2002, KeySpan signed an agreement to sell all 550 acres of the Jamesport land on Long Island's North Shore to the state of New York for $16 million. Governor George Pataki announced that the state had agreed to buy the land through its Environmental Protection Fund. The state in turn would hand the property over to the Trust for Public Land and the Peconic Land Trust, which would oversee the creation of a state park and public beach. The state also plans to sell 300 of the acres to farmers but with the agreement that the land can never be resold to developers. In terms of a financial real estate transaction, we clearly could have gotten more if the property had been sold to private developers. I had taken quite a bit of flak from our financial people about this decision, but I was extremely certain that it was the right thing to do.

Our other option had been to take one of several lucrative offers from private developers who had their own ideas about transforming the property into golf courses or luxury homes or a resort. But standing on the beach that day, I knew the property had to be preserved forever in its natural state and given to the public so that people could enjoy what I was seeing for generations to come. Any other option was simply unthinkable.

The property, as it turns out, was the largest undeveloped parcel of land on Long Island Sound. It included 300 acres of farmland and housed the Hallockville Museum Farm, the only farm museum on Long Island. LILCO had owned the land for more than 30 years, intending back in the 1970s, ironically, to build two nuclear power plants on the site. Back then, such a controversial concept was rejected by the state, and the property had been lying empty and mostly untouched ever since. However, it was costing the company $700,000 annually in property taxes. Our income from the property was $10,000 a year in rent from two Greek potato farmers. Clearly, we needed to do something about it.

David Manning had spent two years working with environmental groups, local town governments, and the governor's office to work out a viable plan for the sale of the land. We hadn't realized when we merged with LILCO that we were acquiring such a pristine parcel and that it would bring along attendant political and economic controversy.

To be honest, I wasn't very aware of the property until I started getting phone calls from a Long Island businessman in 1999. He had accumulated $45 million that he wanted to use to build an exclusive golf course and resort. He wanted to buy the Jamesport property from us.

David, a Canadian and a veteran of environmental issues in the energy industry, convinced me that the plan was something we should reject. Even though I had only seen photographs of the property at that point, I completely agreed. But the businessman was very tenacious. He wanted the property badly and exerted a lot of pressure. But I knew this wasn't the best use of the land. Long Island has more than its share of golf courses already. David pointed out that most of the shoreline of Long Island is privately owned. Only 10 miles of Long Island's 200 miles of coastline are accessible to the public!

Over the next 18 months, the businessman looked elsewhere for his golf course and we considered many other options for the land. One night in Manhattan, David and I attended a fund-raising event at the Waldorf-Astoria. We were quietly making our way to the exit when I stopped to congratulate the honoree for the evening. He took me by the shoulders and asked, "Bob, how old are you?" Surprised, I told him my age, and he laughed. "Well, you must be getting old because you just walked right past Miss Universe." I turned and sure enough, there was the newly crowned Miss Universe standing behind me. Trying to undo my faux pas, I went over to say hello, and Donald Trump stepped forward and said, "Bob, great to see you. I want to buy that piece of property of yours on Long Island."

Donald had apparently talked to our real estate people about the Jamesport property. We had a long business relationship with his father, who owned a great deal of commercial real estate in Brooklyn. Trump's first reaction to our real estate people was to say, "My people don't go to the North Shore. They go to the South Shore." But when he realized how big and spectacular the parcel was, he envisioned a Trump-style resort and golf course. I could just see the gold letters 20 feet high along Sound Avenue in Jamesport. I suggested he call David, and David gave him a business card. Fortunately, he never called so we never had to say no.

My decision about the land wasn't as simple as it might have seemed. Though many suggested I simply give the land to the state, I couldn't do that. The property was owned by our shareholders and I had a responsibility to them as well. We wanted to find a way to do the right thing for all the constituencies involved; to be environmentally sensitive but provide for the financial good of the shareholders.

David handled the negotiations and planning, navigating through the political and financial minefields that often accompany such unusual deals. He pointed out correctly that even if we wanted to sell to developers, to get it approved and to change zoning laws so that houses could be built would be a 10-year-long legal fight and that we'd alienate every environmental group in the region. Since our business is building power plants and laying gas pipes, the environmentalists are our partners, and it is a critical partnership to be maintained.

I convened a special board meeting to announce our plan. We would sell the land for a bargain price of $16 million to the state. Of that, $1.5 million would go to the local communities to cover lost taxes. We would have net proceeds of $14.5 million, which was below the appraised value. But the long-term value to our corporate image and reputation would be priceless. We would truly establish ourselves out on Long Island as a company that cares. When customers thought about KeySpan, those thoughts would likely be favorable. And most of all, we could sleep well at night knowing we did the right thing.

I got some pressure from people inside the company whose job is to look strictly at the bottom line. They pushed to put out a request for proposal (RFP) and to get the highest price we could. One of the board members looked at David and said, "You're the best. You're selling the land for below market value and you made us think it's a bargain."

In truth, it *was* a bargain. When we announced the sale, the media coverage was uniformly positive. The *New York Times* wrote,

> The sale by the KeySpan Energy Corporation is being widely acclaimed by environmentalists. Planners are commending KeySpan, a publicly traded utility, for making a deal that probably realized less in cash than it would have garnered in a sale to developers. "There are not that many organizations that would make a bargain sale with the government," said Robert Pirani, director of environmental projects for the Regional Plan Association, an 80-year-old nonprofit independent research, planning, and advocacy organization. "No doubt they are getting a tax break, but they would have gotten a lot more revenue in development."

To be honest, I'm faced with far tougher decisions almost every day. In this incredibly challenging economy, the strain of balancing between self-interest and enlightened self-interest becomes increasingly difficult. In retrospect, the Jamesport decision was literally a day at the beach, a decision that made itself.

The Monk

~

*B*eing of service to others is not the domain of monks alone.

Pauline Corbett is a KeySpan employee in the company's customer call center and a longtime union member. Raised in North Carolina and transplanted to New York, she has a heart as big as the South. Pauline knows firsthand how difficult it can be to satisfy customer complaints. She spends hours on the phone every workday, making appointments, solving billing problems, and offering assistance.

Pauline believes deeply in the idea of service. As Martin Luther King Jr. said, "Everybody can be great . . . because anybody can serve. You don't have to have a college degree to serve. You don't have to make your subject and verb agree to serve. You only need a heart full of grace, a soul generated by love."

Pauline has such a soul and has lived her life this way, often going beyond her job to do more for others. She built her career on Dr. King's ideal. She and her co-workers banded together to try to make life at the call center more spirited and comfortable.

In order to serve their customers better, Pauline and her group reasoned, they would be aided by periodically taking a break from the endless ringing of telephones and the grind of customer requests. What they needed was a place of solitude and peace. After a few minutes of quiet and calm, they could then return to their jobs refreshed. Near their office in the bustling streets of downtown Brooklyn, such an oasis was tough to find.

Pauline took the initiative. "If there's not a space for quiet around here, why not create one?" she thought. She decided to designate a Morale Team to help improve the situation. Working with their supervisor, the group created a Quiet Room smack in the middle of the hustle and bustle of call center activities. A small conference room on the 16th floor at MetroTech, KeySpan's headquarters in Brooklyn, was designated as the Quiet Room. It was furnished on a shoestring budget from Ikea. Volunteers came from all corners of the company to assist.

They transformed the cold, sterile conference room into a place with Zen-like qualities of peace and tranquility. Warm watercolor screens painted by a fellow employee were placed strategically around the room, providing small private spaces. The room was painted in soft, muted colors, and lush plants were installed to bring in the feeling of nature. A machine that imitated sounds of the ocean was purchased to heighten the tranquil effect.

Harried employees could visit this sanctuary of diffused light and oversized pillows during their breaks. Some would use part of their lunchtime for meditation, reflection, or personal prayer. A co-worker named Angel Flecha, a Zen master in his own right, offered to teach meditation, relaxation, and stress reduction programs to interested staff. Employees could arrive early to take classes, and the company partly subsidized their efforts.

The end result was remarkable: an immediate improvement in call center performance, employee morale, and spiritual energy in the workplace. Employees were refreshed, renewed, and more engaged in company business as well as their personal and spiritual development. Heart and soul mixed with customer calls and billing complaints. It was seamless and integrated.

At one of my "take it for what it's worth" sessions with Bob, I spoke about the Morale Team, the Quiet Room, and the passion of these employees. Bob was moved. I invited him to meet with the team, visit the room, and congratulate the employees for their efforts. When Bob showed up, employees spoke glowingly of their accomplishments and even invited him to spend five minutes of "executive silence" in the Quiet Room. Bob, with his relentless energy and enthusiasm, was only able to endure three minutes. "That's the most solitude I've had in my entire career," he warmly complained when he emerged from the room.

Bob complimented them for both their commitment to the business and their personal values. "Creating a space for peace and quiet in the midst of call center activity helps the business and the people," he said. The group felt recognized and affirmed for their efforts. It was yet another example of how good things happened when Bob left the executive floor and made personal contact with the troops. "This should be replicated," was my thought in leaving that meeting.

Pauline's Morale Team was not alone. The company had many such ad hoc groups of employees who joined together for some worthwhile purpose, buoyed by a similar commitment to perform their work in a more enlightened and engaging manner. These were people of faith and passion, practical people committed to improvement. They were motivated not merely by the money, but by the possibility of bringing greater meaning to their work lives.

"How might we make this company a more inviting and engaging place in which to work?" was a question that resonated in the souls of many employees I met. They reminded me of the alchemists of old, magical people who saw a trace of the divine in the commonplace; early scientists who transformed dross into gold. These were employees who comported themselves in their daily tasks with a sense of the sacred. Of course, they didn't show it religiously—only humanly. They were workers who took stress and changed it into peacefulness with a purpose. They were supervisors who took tarnished and recalcitrant employees and turned them into corporate gold: polished performers and committed staff.

I wanted to maintain momentum and showcase the efforts of these teams, and I wanted Bob to see it. I also wanted our corporate alchemists to be recognized.

In our next meeting, I made Bob an offer he couldn't refuse: support company teamwork, meet employees face-to-face, and get himself out of the executive suite to mingle with the people. I created an "Alchemist Award," a program of monthly meetings with various company teams.

Rather than meet in the auditorium, we met in a conference room seated in a circle. The chosen teams received tiny mounted alchemist hats as their trophies along with certificates for magical teamwork. They then had an opportunity to meet personally and informally with Bob to talk about their accomplishments. And finally, we served a gourmet cake topped with a sorcerer's hat and Merlin wand, cut and served by Bob himself.

"By working as a team and doing your ordinary jobs in extraordinary ways, you've become modern-day alchemists for the company," Bob told each group. Again, the recognition from the CEO had a dramatic impact. One of our young meter readers said to me at the end of her session: "I was surprised to see an executive take such a personal interest in our work. And he seemed to truly understand everything we talked about. He's an okay guy." Almost 50 teams comprising 350 employees attended these events over the course of more than a year.

Bob's response to employee excellence didn't always surface in formal ways and in public forums. Often, through his conversations with me as well as others, he would hear of additional employees who went beyond the call of duty to help a customer, service an account, or perform a hidden act of kindness. Bob referred to these employees as "unsung heroes." While the company had many reward and recognition programs in place, he understood that no program could adequately capture the employee commitment that was out there.

Most of our workers are just average people with families and personal lives, striving to do their ordinary work in extraordinary ways. Bob often asked me to get the phone numbers of these noteworthy employees. When he had a few spare minutes in the day, he'd call them and offer his personal thanks for a job well done. The conversations, while brief, were powerful. Most employees were shocked to receive a personal call from the CEO acknowledging their good efforts.

One of our mechanics told me after receiving one such call, "I can't believe I got a phone call from Catell. He couldn't track me down at work, so he called my home. I almost had a heart attack when my wife told me that it was the chairman on the phone. I thought for a moment that I was getting fired. But somehow he heard about the help I gave to one of our customers and he just wanted to personally thank me. That's what I like about this company. They really do care about the work you do."

Commonly, the employee would react with disbelief, thinking it was a colleague engaged in a workplace spoof. Many times, Bob would hear, "Yeah, sure. The chairman is calling me. Right. Do you think I was born yesterday?" Sometimes Bob wound up spending more time confirming his identity than in complimenting the employee. Once convinced, these employees were genuinely thrilled to receive a call with such a personal touch.

My experience in working in the company was that employees often had a lot more to offer than the normal course of business acknowledged or invited. In my work with Bob, I also sought to find new and different ways of surfacing this energy and creativity, as well as connecting it all to the exercise of business. Bob likewise believed that workers had a wealth of talent to offer, far beyond what was required in their meager job descriptions. How to uncover that creativity in a business setting is something all executives grapple with. I had spent many years in the church seeking this kind of energy, but for a different purpose. With Bob, I was constantly on the lookout for new opportunities to address this challenge.

One opportunity arrived in the form of a request by Bob to host an executive evening meeting designed to explore the company's vision as it marched into the throes of deregulation. Normally, these executive sessions involved a PowerPoint presentation by an officer in the corporate auditorium, followed by a social hour of drinks and appetizers in an executive conference room.

I suggested a daring alternative. We would move the meeting out of the static auditorium, where chairs are bolted to the floor, and transfer it to the company cafeteria with small, intimate tables dispersed throughout the room. Instead of serving food and wine afterward, we'd do it during the program, so executives could ponder, drink, and talk informally with each other. Rather than a staid PowerPoint presentation, we'd create a corporate mural together on a large wall-sized canvas.

While creativity may not come naturally to executives, accountants, and engineers, I believed it was there nonetheless. It merely required some coaxing to surface. I wanted to get everyone to engage his or her own creativity and artistic talents to help fashion a collective view of our future.

While some thought the idea preposterous, Bob wholeheartedly endorsed it. "Do you have any concerns that it won't work out?" Bob asked me before giving his final blessing.

"If I was able to help a 2,000-year-old church re-create itself, assisting a 100-year-old utility to try something new shouldn't be all that difficult," was my response. But in my heart, I knew I couldn't guarantee success. As with any risky venture of this sort, I realized that I could merely invite their participation. Ultimately, the audience would decide whether they wanted the event to be a success. My contribution would be to play the role of a corporate midwife: show up, offer encouragement, and assist in the birthing process.

As the session began, I had 100 corporate leaders before me, seated in bistro-style tables with food and drinks in hand. Bob's introduction gave legitimacy to the venue, and I stepped forward into the corporate unknown. After asking them to momentarily put their drinks aside, I used all my priestly charm to invite them into a moment's meditation about the company's future.

"Our business is changing, and a new future awaits us," I said solemnly, "one that will need to be created not by consultants, but by us. And we are the ones eminently qualified for the task at hand. The answers reside not outside ourselves, but deep within our collective communal selves."

I asked them to take a meditative moment to capture their view of the company's future. For some, I might as well have asked them to don a tutu and perform *Swan Lake*. "Don't worry if you've never meditated before," I compassionately said. "I've done it for many years and will walk you through the process." As some closed their eyes and meditated, others smirked. A few joined in silent recriminations. Being a midwife is never an easy task, but Bob held firm and joined in. To his credit, Bob willingly and even enthusiastically participated in many of my craziest schemes. Only a man at peace with himself and his leadership role could overcome the fears of embarrassment to such an extent. His participation gave legitimacy to what I was doing.

Emerging from the meditation, the group joined me near the blank canvas where our corporate artist awaited. The group was uneasy and unsure, nascent artists in suits and ties. With a minimum of prodding, they suggested images to the artist. Many offered explicit detail and colorful imagery. In an air of creative inspiration and excitement, their words were transformed into images on the larger-than-life canvas before them. Quickly, there appeared mountains to be scaled, rivers to be crossed, prizes to be won.

Pictures of executives extending helping hands to willing employees were drawn in. This all took place before me, accompanied by bickering, squabbling, and a smorgasbord of diverse opinions. They challenged, negotiated, and ultimately reached consensus on a corporate work of art.

When it was done, they had given birth to a mural of their own making, a company vision fashioned out of wine, wisdom, and the wealth of a 100-year-old tradition. They were pleased enough to request that the mural remain on the cafeteria wall for another week to allow all employees to see it and offer thoughts and suggestions to shape its final design.

What this demonstrated was that even in a staid utility there was fun to be had and creativity to be expressed. Executives could join artistic hands with employees in crafting a vision of a future company of their own choosing.

This small exercise spawned other creative programs of employee engagement. Executives began to meet informally every month with employees in sessions we called "Straight Talk." Straight Talk provided workers with face-to-face meetings with their corporate leaders to hear fresh business news, discuss corporate change efforts, and calm employee fears. Candor and frankness were encouraged. Workers were invited to write more sensitive questions on index cards before the meeting, to ensure that uncomfortable items got anonymously aired.

Having never worked anywhere else except a monastery, I was less surprised than some about how openly these programs were embraced by both officers and employees at all levels. I had a pretty good idea how unusual our organization was, but for some, this seemed well outside the white lines of business. We were trying to shape Brooklyn Union's future, and we would all soon learn how daunting this journey would become.

CHAPTER FOUR

~

The LILCO Deal

A time to cast away stones, and a time to gather stones together.

—Ecclesiastes

In 1998, Bob Catell prepared to consummate the most important and dramatic deal in his seven-year tenure as CEO. Over the previous several months, he had engineered a merger with Long Island Lighting Company (LILCO), the giant electric and gas utility that served more than one million customers on Long Island and in Queens. At the end of May, the agreement would be signed and a new era would begin.

While any merger is fraught with risk, the LILCO deal was unusually complex and perilous because it involved a complicated third-party arrangement with the state of New York. It also involved a partnership with LILCO's chairman, an imposing executive named William Catacosinos. Catell believed that he had established a strong relationship with Catacosinos and could work together with him on a transaction that made perfect business sense for both companies. He was wary but optimistic. He had no idea of the drama that would unfold in the coming months, testing his leadership skills as never before.

If Catell had trepidations about the deal with LILCO, he kept his concerns to himself. He believed that a leader had to present a strong and optimistic face for his troops, especially when taking them into new, uncharted territory. Being the ultimate consensus-builder, Catell sought counsel from corporate officers, from the board of directors, and from trusted associates outside the company. He also leaned heavily on an ex-monk.

The unusual but quietly effective partnership between Catell and Kenny Moore flourished through the mid-1990s. Moore spent less time in Catell's office than people imagined, but their connection grew through the countless small successes that Moore accomplished on his mission in search of the corporate soul. Moore had proven his worth by ministering to an endless array of corporate logjams, bringing his unique sensibilities to various groups that had stopped communicating and getting people to open up, talk, and see things from just a slightly different angle. Even the most cynical corporate officers who had rolled their eyes and expressed their skepticism when first hearing of Moore's mission had been won over, not just by Moore's unique personality and perspective, but because he got results.

"Was I cynical? Yeah. I'm a lawyer and lawyers are skeptics by nature," says Steve Zelkowitz, the company's former general counsel. "I thought, 'This is fluff, window dressing. You can't be serious.' But a few years ago, I felt there were some issues building up within the legal department. I suggested we get together to talk about it, air some issues and try to get them resolved, and several people told me that Kenny could handle this. I said, 'These are lawyers. They are guarded. They choose their words very carefully and think about the impact of their words. You're going to have a tough time drawing them out.' But, son of a gun, Kenny was spectacular. He got them to emote, and I saw a side to people I'd never seen before. I mean, people were crying."

Catell, already a believer, wanted Moore to minister to a wider corporate flock. He felt a certain urgency to shake things up. He knew that people were becoming increasingly stuck—frustrated, complacent, cynical, and distracted. There was, within this values-oriented culture, a growing malaise that had been born from a century as a monopoly. This was hardly surprising in a regulated utility where the attrition rate was abnormally low and many long-term employees had a sense of entitlement, like civil servants, whose jobs were safe and untouchable and the work could be mailed in. On top of that, people had begun to notice the suddenly robust economy with its lure of new, perhaps more lucrative opportunities in high tech or telecommunications or investment banking. Rallying the troops in this day and age, even in a heavily engineering-oriented culture, required new kinds of thinking, new ways of looking at the world. Catell knew that he had tapped an invaluable resource in Moore, and he encouraged him to push forward.

At the same time, Catell understood that the company could not remain as it had been. Something had to give. Having saturated its current territory and with the onset of deregulation, Brooklyn Union, despite its stellar reputation and deep commitment to its stakeholders, would slowly devolve into irrelevancy unless it considered dramatic changes. In 1996, Catell led the effort to convince the Public Service Commission to approve the creation of a separate holding company, which would open the door for entry into unregulated, competitive markets such as energy services. He had named the holding company KeySpan Energy Corporation.

Driven by the advent of the Internet and new technologies, even the staid energy industry was morphing into hot new markets, such as energy trading. And not unlike other industries facing deregulation, there was pressure within the energy industry for consolidation. With nimble, intense competitors like Enron changing all the rules, companies like Brooklyn Union were suddenly appearing, in the business community's eyes, as quaint, dated players mired in another era.

Catell, with a fiscal responsibility to his shareholders, had to at least entertain the notion of selling Brooklyn Union to a bigger player with deeper pockets. But that course was at direct odds with his vision: to grow Brooklyn Union into the most powerful energy company in the Northeast.

So Catell explored several options. The one that seemed most intriguing was growth through acquisition, and the most desirable candidate was in his own backyard. LILCO was a merger or acquisition waiting to happen and had been for a long time. As far back as 1984, Brooklyn Union had approached LILCO about acquiring its small but potent gas properties. LILCO's chairman, Catacosinos, then new to his post but already known for his aggressive management style, rejected the offer.

At the time, Gene Luntey, then Brooklyn Union's CEO, made an uncharacteristically bold and risky move. Wanting access to a vast untapped market for gas customers on Long Island and believing that the financially strapped LILCO could use the cash, Luntey bypassed Catacosinos and approached LILCO's board directly with his offer. An angry Catacosinos convinced his board to reject the offer, which resulted in a rift between the once friendly companies that lasted several years.

Not long after El Larson became CEO of KeySpan and Catell was elevated to chief operating officer, they agreed that the animosity between the two utilities was foolish and unnecessary. Larson reached out to Catacosinos and suggested a meeting to seek détente. Catacosinos graciously agreed, and the bad feelings were apparently laid to rest. Over the next few years, with cordial relations in place, Catell would periodically revisit the idea of obtaining LILCO's gas business. Catacosinos was steadfast in his refusal. He saw the gas business as a nice, if small, cash cow and had no desire to give it up.

But all was not well on Long Island and hadn't been for many years. LILCO, under Catacosinos, had struggled financially due to the Shoreham nuclear power plant debacle that had burdened the company for more than a decade. In the early 1970s, LILCO had begun construction of a nuclear power plant in Shoreham on Long Island's North Shore. When the Three Mile Island meltdown occurred in March 1979, the public's perception of nuclear power plants went from wariness to outright fear. And if Three Mile Island was in a relatively rural part of Pennsylvania, Shoreham was smack in the middle of the densely populated Long Island with its more than 2.5 million residents. A disaster there would be catastrophic, and the Three Mile Island accident galvanized local opposition against Shoreham.

Still under construction, Shoreham was forced to install new safety equipment that sharply jacked up the cost. Though it was completed at a cost of $5.5 billion, the Shoreham plant was never put into service due to the overwhelming opposition on Long Island. Nevertheless, the plant had run test operations which ended up being a costly decision because once running, the plant could not be deconstructed and sold off for materials and equipment.

Thus, LILCO was forced to carry a $5.5 billion debt on its books and search elsewhere for electric power. The result was that electricity rates on Long Island rose substantially throughout the 1980s and 1990s. The rates were more than double the national average and the highest in the continental United States. Though LILCO was an efficient organization with skilled and dedicated employees, the company became reviled on Long Island and Catacosinos emerged as the main villain.

Public criticism focused on Catacosinos' relentless push to complete the Shoreham plant despite local opposition as well as the deal he made with then governor Mario Cuomo to close the plant and pass the costs on to customers through exorbitant electricity rates. The criticism would rise with each new rate hike as well as other isolated incidents. He earned customers' wrath, for example, when he refused to cut short a vacation in Italy while Long Island residents were left without power in the aftermath of Hurricane Gloria in 1985. LILCO employees were painted with the same broad brush, and for many employees the solution was to simply avoid telling neighbors and new acquaintances where they worked.

And as usually happens, Shoreham and LILCO's higher electricity rates became a political football. In 1986, Cuomo and the New York State Legislature had created a state agency called the Long Island Power Authority (LIPA) with the intent to take over the Shoreham plant and possibly even LILCO itself. But Cuomo could not persuade Republican legislators to approve his plan, and he found a formidable adversary in Catacosinos. Catacosinos had his own ideas about where the priorities lay and as long as he maintained shareholder value, he was unmoved by the continuing maelstrom. Beyond that, LIPA was never able to gain public support for the government to take over a private company.

By 1994, electric rates on Long Island became a linchpin issue in the gubernatorial election. In October, a desperate Cuomo proposed a complete state takeover of LILCO. It was not enough. Promising to decrease rates by "double digits" and deriding Cuomo's takeover plan as "misguided," the Republican George Pataki ousted the once popular Cuomo, which was considered a major upset in a heavily Democratic state.

Not surprisingly, Pataki found the LILCO situation as confounding as his predecessor had. Ironically, he eventually proposed a plan for the state to take over LILCO that was essentially the same as the Cuomo plan.

Catell watched the LILCO drama unfold with great interest. He hatched an idea that he believed might resolve the Long Island dilemma and benefit Brooklyn Union at the same time. In the summer of 1997, Catell approached Catacosinos and suggested what he called a "public/private partnership." Rather than simply buying LILCO's gas properties, Brooklyn Union and LILCO would merge. The new entity, as yet unnamed, would take over the gas systems and power plants, and the state, through LIPA, would borrow $7.3 billion of tax-exempt debt to buy LILCO's electric transmission and distribution system. In turn, LIPA would enter a deal in which the newly merged company would run the electric business for LIPA under a long-term agreement.

LIPA was in a position to take on LILCO's massive debt, which would essentially wipe the Shoreham debt from LILCO's books, because the state agency could borrow through tax-exempt bonds, thus refinancing LILCO's debt at a low interest rate. LIPA, as a state agency, does not pay income taxes, and it doesn't have shareholders so it isn't burdened paying dividends. The governor, Catell suggested, would undoubtedly welcome the deal because he could finally deliver on his promise to dramatically lower electricity rates on Long Island. Brooklyn Union's stellar reputation among lawmakers and regulators offset the bad feeling and passion that ran against LILCO, thus making the deal palatable to a wide coalition.

Catacosinos was an astute businessman. He had a Ph.D. in Economics and preferred to be called Dr. Catacosinos. He saw the plan as a way to wipe the onerous debt off his balance sheet forever. His shareholders would be ecstatic that he had engineered a new, financially stable company that would be able to maximize earnings far into the future. After the usual political wrangling, the governor approved the deal and set the agreement in motion.

Despite some misgivings, shareholders of both companies approved the merger. Over the next few months, Catell and his executive team held meetings with Catacosinos and LILCO to facilitate the merger. Working out the political kinks with the state was a cakewalk compared to the complex negotiations of creating a brand-new company out of two existing entities, especially entities with such vastly different cultures. If Brooklyn Union was familial, its employees empowered and proud of their employer, LILCO was the classic command-and-control environment.

Catell understood the trauma he was unleashing within Brooklyn Union. More than a century into its existence, the company was now going to be transformed into something new and unknown. Though it was intended as a merger of equals, LILCO was nearly twice the size of Brooklyn Union. Since many Brooklyn Union employees, including Catell himself, lived on Long Island, LILCO's reputation was well known around Brooklyn headquarters. The great corporate millstone—fear, uncertainty, and doubt—immediately gripped Brooklyn Union's population, and both Catell and Kenny Moore understood that if ever divine intervention was needed, now would be the time.

While Catell believed he understood the magnitude of his bold step, he was quite unprepared for the surprises that lay ahead.

The CEO

*A*nyone who has been involved in a significant corporate merger knows how daunting such a venture can be. Getting through the endless financial and legal issues can lead to sleepless nights and a run on Rolaids. But confronting the cultural issues and building a brand-new company from two existing organizations is an intricate experience that can't be gleaned from a textbook. I wouldn't recommend any of this for the faint of heart.

So I admit that I did not have a significant merger on my resume when I set out to do the LILCO deal. What I did have was the conviction that this was the linchpin for Brooklyn Union's future. I am not somebody who acts on gut instinct alone, and I considered the ramifications of this merger for a long time before we finally pulled the trigger. The senior executive team was with me. I had the support of my board as well as some of my most trusted advisers, people like Fred Lowther, a lawyer who had assisted us with difficult legal issues in the past.

Because of the involvement with the state of New York and LIPA, the negotiations to consummate the deal were especially long and complex. The original deal was engineered by Frank Zarb, then chairman of LIPA. Shortly thereafter, Zarb stepped down and was replaced by Richard Kessel as chairman of LIPA.

We negotiated a deal in which LIPA would buy the electric transmission and distribution system owned by LILCO. The new company, formed by the merger of Brooklyn Union and LILCO, would own LILCO's electric power plants and its gas properties and it would manage the transmission and distribution of electricity for LIPA under contract for eight years. It was an odd, somewhat cumbersome way to do business, but it was the best financial solution to an otherwise insurmountable problem. We believed that the state would honor its commitment to take over LILCO's debt, and that is, in fact, what it did.

At the same time, Bill Catacosinos and I began negotiating what form the new company would take. As in any merger, we had to figure out who the corporate officers would be, the makeup of a board of directors, and the multiple layers of corporate hierarchy.

Bill was very insistent that he be named chairman and CEO of the new company. I was not surprised at his stance. He was simply not the kind of person who would have accepted the number two position in an organization. If LILCO was a command-and-control type environment, it was clear that Bill was the commander and controller.

The Brooklyn Union board was not pleased with this arrangement and insisted that I be named president and chief operating officer of the new company. And more important, they also insisted that the agreement state clearly that Bill would relinquish the CEO title to me in a year. After that, he would stay on for an indefinite period as chairman.

As someone who was already a CEO, I wasn't thrilled with the prospect of becoming second in command. I felt, though, that I could manage it for a year as long as it was clearly defined and articulated in writing when I would take over as CEO. I had a verbal commitment from Bill that he would stay on as chairman for only a year or two beyond that.

Keep in mind that Bill and I had established a very cordial relationship by that point in time. We weren't close friends but we had a good personal relationship. We'd socialized together with our wives on several occasions. Bill could be a very charming and personable guy. Mostly, I believed that he respected me and that my influence was being felt.

He was also a tough negotiator and he worked very hard to position his people with key roles and responsibilities. Since in reality we were acquiring LILCO's stock and paying a modest premium for it, I felt we should be in the driver's seat. Yet I also understood that this was a partnership and that the only way the partnership could succeed would be with a strong sense of trust between us. You have to make compromises in any significant deal. I worked hard to protect my people and make sure they were taken care of with positions of responsibility. But as I said earlier, mergers are not for the faint of heart. Bill was smart, tough, and a good negotiator.

For example, I believed we should call the new company KeySpan Energy. It was a strong, inclusive name that we had used for our holding company for two years. But Bill simply wouldn't agree to that. He had one of his advertising people come up with an alternative and we ended up, much to my chagrin, with the name MarketSpan. It was a compromise. I knew it wasn't great. Again, I felt that in any merger such as this, compromises had to be made.

Yet with all that, I knew this merger was the right thing to do. I knew that Brooklyn Union could not allow a competitor to come in and acquire LILCO. Long Island was very important to our future. This was a strategic move and I believed it would be worth the pain.

Among the most important decisions we had to make was the creation of a new board of directors. We agreed that the new board would include 15 directors: six from LILCO, six from Brooklyn Union, and three new outside directors whom we would mutually agree upon.

We each had a number of new candidates for the board, and on the Friday morning of Memorial Day weekend, I arranged for one of my candidates to meet with Bill and me for breakfast. This was May 22. The closing of the merger was slated for May 28, the following Thursday.

When we arrived at the Garden City Hotel on Long Island, we received a message that our candidate's schedule had been inadvertently mixed up and he was unable to make the breakfast meeting. I suggested that Bill and I take the opportunity to tie up some loose ends before the closing.

Over breakfast, Bill looked at me and said, "Oh, by the way, Bob, there's a matter that you should be aware of. When this transaction takes place, I'm eligible for a payout under a change of control provision in my contract."

"Well, we all have change of control clauses," I replied. "That's not unusual."

"No," he told me. "You don't understand. Not only am I eligible but this deal *triggers* the change of control."

I couldn't believe what I was hearing. "Bill," I said, "that's not what a change of control is all about." As most executives understand, such clauses in their contracts are triggered only when they are to leave the company. Bill was staying on as chairman and CEO.

"I can't believe you are telling me this now, on the Friday before the closing," I said. He pointed out that he had a legal opinion to substantiate his action, an opinion he had never shared with me.

"Give me the order of magnitude here. What kind of dollars are we talking about?" I asked him.

"Well, in my case, I have a retirement package that also gets triggered here so I get paid that, too," he replied. He told me that he would receive about $8 million for his salary and bonus. Then he added that his entire group of corporate officers, 26 in all, were also entitled to payouts as well, totaling about $5 million.

My head was spinning but I maintained an outward calm. I told Bill that I was upset that he hadn't shared any of this with me before and that once this became public, it would set off a political and public relations furor. He responded by telling me that he believed that any public reaction would be short-lived and that he and his executive team were contractually entitled to the payments.

As we prepared to leave, I said, "Bill, I think you're wrong on this one. I'm afraid this could really jeopardize your position as well as the future of the new company."

When I left the meeting, I got on the phone and immediately called back to Brooklyn. I alerted the executive team as to what happened and then called our legal adviser Fred Lowther. Fred would become the chief strategist in addressing this new issue.

We called for an emergency board meeting on Wednesday afternoon, two days after Memorial Day, to figure out what to do. In the meantime, I reviewed the legal opinion prepared by LILCO's law firm. LILCO's general counsel produced a letter from a New York law firm dated April 1998 that stated that the purchase of LILCO by LIPA was deemed a change of control and triggered a payment. Our lawyers had never seen this letter before. I knew that my board would not take this well at all, and I could only imagine the reaction at LIPA and at the governor's office in Albany.

My anger and frustration were building but there was yet another shock awaiting me. The $8 million Bill had mentioned was just a small part of his package. That represented just his compensation package. When you added his retirement package, the total came to $42 million! And the amount going to his executives totaled another $25 million! What came to light was that this had all been approved—reluctantly, I might add—by the LILCO board just *10 days* before the closing of our deal. The press reported that Bill had unsuccessfully demanded $63 million for himself but the board balked at that amount. Minutes from that meeting showed that the LILCO board did not want to give him this compensation package but they feared that if they refused, the dispute would become public and threaten to destroy the merger. They settled on the $42 million and kept the dispute private.

The result was that, unbeknownst to me, we were creating a merger that would pay the new CEO and his executive team millions for the privilege of closing the deal! They were still going to be employees and collect their paychecks, benefits, and pensions.

When our board met in Brooklyn on Wednesday afternoon, there was a sense of betrayal and disbelief. The obvious urge was to scuttle the deal and walk away. But it was a delicate situation because the merger remained critical for the company. The board did not want to do anything that was detrimental to Brooklyn Union shareholders. And even though technically the payments Catacosinos would receive would come from the LILCO shareholders, those shareholders were about to become shareholders in the new company. So I had a responsibility to them as well. Further, there was the legal issue. If Catacosinos and his officers were indeed legally entitled to the money, our decision to walk away could potentially be construed as a breach of contract and we could be sued.

At the end of a difficult meeting, we concluded that the risk of *not* going forward was greater than the risk of going forward with the transaction.

So on May 28, after an all-night session poring over hundreds of legal documents and enough paper to cover two long maple conference tables, we put on neatly pressed suits and smiles and headed to LIPA's Uniondale, Long Island, headquarters to sign the agreement. In front of the governor and the press, Bill and I clasped hands and, along with LIPA's chairman, Richard Kessel, mugged for the cameras and effectively brought an end to the storied histories of two very different companies. Brooklyn Union's 103 years and LILCO's 87 years as independent companies were over. Kessel called it "an historic moment for Long Island." Bill expressed his sadness at the end of a bittersweet saga and managed to toss in a dig at the "political environment and the errors of the past," referring to LILCO's 24-year struggle with the Shoreham nuclear power plant debacle.

The good news was that LIPA was able to immediately announce significant electricity rate cuts for Long Island residents and promise refund checks by September. We finished talking with the media and headed to Wall Street, where we rang the closing bell to conclude that day's trading on the New York Stock Exchange. We ended the day with champagne and chocolate-covered strawberries, along with toasts to the new enterprise.

MarketSpan, a name that would have a dramatically short life, had been born. I was exhausted, relieved, anxious, and worried all at the same time. What should have been a joyous day in my business career instead left me with an uneasy feeling of ambivalence and trepidation. As I said good-bye to Bill, I felt betrayed and personally outraged that he had seemingly undermined a trusting relationship. I sensed that the goodwill of the merger would soon be tainted by the revelations of his payout and that the new company might be terribly damaged by this news.

I knew that this issue, while an internal matter, would eventually leak out to the press and set off a firestorm. I thought, among other things, that I should talk to Kenny and think about ways to prepare our employees for some extra trauma, added to the trauma they were already experiencing.

Memorial Day signaled the beginning of summer, which had always been a relatively quiet time in the gas business. I couldn't forecast the future, but I was reasonably sure that this would be the hottest summer I had ever experienced.

The Monk

While I'm no whiz kid regarding mergers and acquisitions, I was well aware that most of them ended up as failures, and not because they had a wrong business model or a flawed customer strategy. They failed because the employees somehow got forgotten in the merger process. Workers lost trust in the company's leadership. Employees' hope for a better tomorrow waned. While trust and hope are spiritual qualities, they impact the corporate bottom line—positively and negatively. Bob understood this. A growing number of folks at Brooklyn Union understood this. Some of the leaders at LILCO did not.

The LILCO culture was different. This was a company that for well over a decade struggled on the precipice of financial oblivion while it tried to fund the construction of Shoreham. That financial distress and the austerity budgets that went along with it resulted in a warfare mentality and more of a command-and-control culture.

Brooklyn Union's culture was in sharp contrast. Beloved by the community and prosperous in the marketplace, it had the luxury of encouraging dialogue, fostering differences, and inviting dissent. In this company, executives welcomed a questioning attitude and went out of their way to solicit employee feedback. The input and advice of customers and employees alike frequently shaped decisions. I had come to both inherit this tradition and, with Bob's support, champion its place in the business.

In some regards, a merger is like a marriage. And this one was not made in heaven. Our employees were skeptical of it from the outset but were willing to give Bob and the other executives a period of grace to work out the kinks. I took advantage of this initial window of opportunity to go before the merger transition team and make a proposal for directly including all employees in the merger process.

"We have a strategy for our shareholders and our customers, but we don't have one for our employees," I pointed out to the executive group. I proposed to informally bring together groups of employees from both companies well in advance of the merger's completion. This would provide a chance to start building a unified culture, explore similarities, and initiate an employee feedback mechanism to the merger team at the very beginning of the process.

Although some of the LILCO officers resisted my offer, it was still early in the merger process and our executives prevailed, speaking convincingly about the need for employee involvement. Unfortunately, their ability to compellingly influence major decisions was short-lived and would steadily decline as the merger moved forward.

Once I had the executive committee's approval, regular meetings began to take place immediately under a program that I had christened "Employee Care." Union and management employees from both LILCO and Brooklyn Union came together to meet, discuss operating practices as well as explore common grounds of interest. While skepticism was rampant, I began to see a spark of hope for a shared future. I experienced the LILCO employees as a dedicated group of warm-hearted people who had tremendous resiliency and spirit. They struck me as committed employees caught in the headlights of some bad executive decisions, longing to be released from the harsh media spotlight.

These frequent meetings gave a broad array of Brooklyn Union people a chance to see their counterparts not as some distant enemy to be engaged in battle but rather as fellow employees equally laboring within an inherently flawed system. It also provided LILCO employees an opportunity to raise their concerns in an anonymous fashion. As one Long Island employee told me at the end of a session: "It's refreshing to meet my counterparts and to be able to talk openly about all that's going on. I'm only hoping that it all continues after the merger is complete."

I regularly reported back to the executive team the results of these sessions, summarizing employees' hopes as well as their fears. The Brooklyn Union executives listened with responsive attention. A number of the LILCO leaders merely tolerated my reports and continued to remain skeptical of involving anybody but their handpicked teams in the merger process. The Employee Care sessions made some headway in dispelling the rumors and prejudices that were engulfing both companies as the merger became more strained. But they ultimately proved to be insufficient.

While the results from these public sessions offered some ray of hope, my private meetings with Brooklyn Union employees proved more disquieting. Some of our better employees were starting to jump ship and leave the company in the belief that what was taking place was not a merger of equals, but rather a LILCO takeover. There was also a growing fear that our executives were unresponsive to the pending calamity.

My next "take it for what it's worth" meeting with Bob was a disturbing one. "Employees are starting to lose hope and leave the company," I said. There was unfolding a pervasive groundswell of negative feelings about the merger. Employees were losing trust in the leadership as well as in the future of the company.

Bob listened, and I could tell that he was distressed. "Kenny, there is a lot going on—some of which I'm not free to share with you," he told me. "But I can assure you that we're making solid progress on this deal. I continue to believe that it will all work out fine and be beneficial for our employees as well as theirs. Yet I'm pained to hear that our better employees would want to leave. Any suggestions on what to do?"

I have often observed that a common tendency in corporations is that when harsh realities surface, people want to distance themselves from them. My instinct is to do the opposite. Rather than shy away from the difficulty, I want to get closer to it, investigate and explore it, give it a fair hearing with some room to breathe. From my battle with cancer, I had learned that it is better to openly discuss difficult issues than to keep them locked up inside to fester. The price you pay for this approach is that not all that comes out is pleasant. But it's often medicinal and therapeutic.

With that in mind, I told Bob plainly: "I believe in getting our employees together to air the discussion openly. I'd prefer for you as the CEO to hear it all firsthand. If a few employees have already left the company, I'm sure there are many more considering it."

My suggestion was to host a full day session with 50 of our professional staff to air their hopes and fears about the merger as well as offer some suggestions for making progress. I'd facilitate the session, but I wanted Bob to spend time with the group at the end of the day to hear their thoughts. He pondered this. "Fifty employees? All day long? I'm worried that it might generate a lot of negative energy."

Knowing that he wouldn't like what I was about to say, I spoke bluntly anyway. "Based on what I'm hearing, the negative energy is already out there. And it's widespread. I'd like to use this session as a kind of release valve. Let employees freely speak their mind and get it out of their system. It will create an environment where their concerns could all be put on the table for us to hear and also give senior management an opportunity to respond. While it may not be pleasant, I think it would be helpful. With so much secrecy and mistrust swirling around, it would be a breath of fresh air to speak openly. I'd recommend we do it."

Bob's reply was supportive but he was wary of attending. "My time's not my own these days," he said. "I'm deep in the throes of the merger. I'd fear that if we schedule something, I'll be pulled away at the last moment." Bob asked that Craig Matthews, Brooklyn Union's president, attend the event and report results back to him. Craig had been his right-hand man throughout the merger process.

I was fine with that, but wanted the meeting to take place soon. As I got up to leave, Bob stopped me. "One more unofficial request," he said. "Say a few prayers for me if you get the chance. This merger is playing out differently that I expected and I could use all the help I can get." It would only be months later that I'd come to fully under-

stand the depth of his need and the magnitude of the heavenly support required.

Craig was more than willing to participate in the program. And
rather than rely on words alone to encompass the passion of this
planned event, I once again invited our graphic artist to help capture
all that would flow from the discussion.

A few weeks later, the meeting took place. In a large conference
room emptied of all but 50 chairs, Craig welcomed the group and invited their candor and honesty. He then returned to his office to allow
the group a few hours' time to do their work. Large blank walls were
covered with white paper ready to record their pictorial images on
three aspects of the pending merger: their hopes, fears, and suggestions for managing the merger.

We spent several hours discussing these topics and working with
the artist to record the group's thoughts and feelings onto the white
canvases. The session proved to be more than merely a release valve
of employee concerns. It proved to be a harbinger of things to come.
When Craig returned after lunch, the pictures hung like a stark
Rorschach image of the company's dark state of mind.

Unlike the mural that had materialized at our previous session depicting the company's future as hopeful, engaging, and inviting, these
pictures proved more damning. While the three-part design of the session gave these 50 employees more than enough room to explore their
hopes and suggestions for corporate success, a large part of their attention focused on their anxieties. As Craig sat before the group, the
most prominent mural depicted the prescient fears of the employee
community.

I offered to translate the pictures for Craig, but they pretty much
spoke for themselves. There was Brooklyn Union depicted as the *Ti-
tanic* sinking after striking an iceberg marked LILCO. And there were
several Brooklyn Union executives perilously holding on to a lone life
jacket in the chilly sea, surrounded by fellow employees floating in
shark-infested waters. Craig was not pleased.

"This was not something I was expecting to see," he said, tight-
lipped.

Those in the room spoke candidly about what they saw happening on the merger teams and how they felt things would play out. While Craig acknowledged their concerns, there was a tone of defensiveness in his voice as he sought to understand the depth of their misgivings. But the pictures spoke vividly. Any rebuttal he offered fell upon skeptical ears.

In his closing comments, Craig sought to bolster spirits and assuage fears. He offered his personal commitment to making this a merger of equals. Craig thanked the group for their honesty and left the meeting to share the results with Bob, all with the unstated hope that these disturbing pictures would never become reality.

But the insights and fears of our employees turned out to be well-founded. I watched as events unfolded over the next several months and became certain that regardless of the ultimate outcome, I would soon be calling upon all the skills and wisdom I had gained in the monastery. And I would undoubtedly be busier than I'd ever been in this job.

CHAPTER FIVE

High Noon

Fortune leaves always some door open to come at a remedy.

—Miguel de Cervantes

Within a week of the closing of the Brooklyn Union–LILCO–LIPA merger, the state of New York disclosed to the press the $67 million payout to Catacosinos and his 26 top officers. Catacosinos grossly underestimated what he had predicted would be a "one-day story in *Newsday*." The news set off a firestorm of anger that began in Albany and spread throughout the cities and towns across Long Island. And the story would remain on or near the front page and editorial page all summer long.

"MarketScam!" proclaimed the New York newspapers, parodying the merged company's new name. "The amount going to Mr. Catacosinos is outrageous, especially considering LILCO's poor record as an electricity supplier," intoned an editorial in the *New York Times*.

Among those who were particularly perturbed by the payout was New York governor George Pataki. Pataki had invested a great deal of time and political capital in finding a solution to Long Island's high electricity rates. He had long been frustrated with LILCO. He had also made promises and now, just days after believing he had finally found a workable, long-term solution to the problem, he was greeted by a revelation that would further shock and anger his constituents on Long Island.

One day after state Republicans nominated him for reelection, Pataki launched a blistering attack on Catacosinos, promising an investigation of the LILCO payments and calling for Catacosinos to resign. In a published statement, Pataki said, "Not content with ripping off its own ratepayers for decades, now LILCO's board of directors and management are robbing their shareholders in one extraordinary secret act of greed. It is a sorry finish for a company with a history of disturbing and ill-advised decisions that benefited a select few at the expense of consumers. These payments should not stand. The money should be returned immediately."

The money would not be returned. Despite the thorough vetting by corporate and state attorneys along with threats of investigations, Catacosinos had been careful to make sure his actions were technically legitimate if not popular. In his own defense, Catacosinos believed that he was entitled to the payout. He felt he had salvaged LILCO and its shareholders and had kept the company out of bankruptcy through the Shoreham situation. He had, he believed, saved the company from disaster and he was entitled to be paid for that.

In an interview with *Newsday*, Catacosinos claimed he was being unfairly portrayed as "a grubby, greedy person always taking money. In my judgment that's not true." He said, "I've worked hard. I've done my job and the result has been that I received a benefit based on a contract that was in place in 1984. People may not be happy with the amount and the result, but that's what the contract called for." He added that he'd done nothing secretive. "They had the information," he told *Newsday*. "It was available to them. If they were interested, they would have done their homework."

Given the timing, the late 1990s, when the bounds of corporate greed and astronomical CEO compensation packages had reached beyond anyone's imagination, Catacosinos had some reason to wonder what the fuss was all about. He said that executives routinely got such fat payouts when their companies merged, and many of his peers were far more highly paid than he. "It's as if all of this has never happened before," he told *Newsday*.

Believing the storm would eventually blow over, Catacosinos tried to assume control of MarketSpan and work through the chaotic aftermath of his payout revelation. But the presence of New York State in the deal made any forward progress next to impossible. Rather than dissipate, the heat intensified as calls for his resignation proliferated and battle lines got drawn.

LIPA's chairman, Richard Kessel, rebutted Catacosinos' explanation as "completely false." After meeting with LIPA's board, Kessel announced that the unexpected payout "will have far-reaching consequences for MarketSpan," including penalties and a decreasing likelihood of future cooperation. "This message sends a strong signal to MarketSpan that its biggest customer is seriously dissatisfied," Kessel stated. "These payments were a serious breach of our agreement and they were deliberately concealed."

With investigations getting underway by the U.S. Justice Department, the New York Public Service Commission, and the New York attorney general's office, the inevitable shareholder lawsuits soon followed. "It was an unbelievable mess," recalls Fred Lowther, the lead attorney on the case for Catell and Brooklyn Union.

Meanwhile, inside the former Brooklyn Union, there was turmoil. This new turn of events sent shock waves across an organization already fearful of what the merger would mean for their jobs and their corporate culture. Most Brooklyn Union veterans couldn't imagine working for a company with a culture like LILCO's.

Trying to live up to its part of the bargain and share the leadership of the merged company with LILCO, Brooklyn Union had offered change-of-control severance packages to several senior-level people, talented officers who would be missed. For those who remained, the integration of the two companies became a nightmarish guessing game: who would keep their jobs in the new company and who would lose.

There was a pervasive feeling around the halls and cubicles in Brooklyn that Brooklyn Union's culture would not emerge from the

merger intact. Needless to say, Kenny Moore found himself in con-
stant demand. He organized a series of employee meetings designed to
allow people to express their fears, share their concerns, and vent
their anger.

He couldn't help but remember the gathering the previous winter
at Brooklyn Union in which the company artist drew a giant mural
depicting the feelings and fears of those in the room. Those drawings
had come eerily to life.

During the summer months of June and July, the fear, uncertainty, and doubt in Brooklyn reached a fever pitch. "The employees
sensed something bad was going to happen," said Maurice Shaw, senior vice president of corporate affairs, who has since retired. "There
were some of us who knew if things happened as we anticipated, we'd
be without jobs."

During the integration, Moore was called upon to make a presentation to an integration meeting that included Catacosinos, Catell,
and their respective senior officers. Bob Fani, who was then a Brooklyn Union senior vice president, recalls walking into the meeting and
seeing the former Brooklyn Union officers seated on one side of the
table, their LILCO counterparts on the other. Fani thought to himself, "This isn't going to be a team anytime soon." He turned out to be
right. Subsequent senior-level meetings found each side camped
across the conference table from each other, a sense of "us versus
them" the pervasive feeling in the room.

At that first gathering, Kenny spoke to the group about his work
and his desire to build a team from within this new organization. He
employed his usual mix of humor, wit, and wisdom drawn from his
work within Brooklyn Union in a furtive attempt at opening lines of
communications and creating some bonds. Catacosinos and his officers seemed amused and intrigued by Moore, having never experienced anything like him in their own careers.

"But as soon as Kenny left, you could feel things change," Fani recalls. "The dynamics in the room changed just like that. It was obvious that some of the LILCO people thought that what Kenny was
doing was a joke and they weren't always laughing with him. And that

bothered the Brooklyn Union officers because we understood the value Kenny brings. We were concerned whether or not the Brooklyn Union leadership would be willing to stay and work in an environment that seemed like it had the potential to lose the values that we'd grown to know and love."

Elaine Weinstein, the head of corporate human resources, had been with the company only a short time when the merger process got underway. She became a major figure in the integration process of the two companies and faced the daunting task of merging two remarkably different cultures. Clearly, LILCO's autocratic, top-down leadership approach did not meld with the congenial, consensus-driven model at Brooklyn Union. And for Weinstein, the only way to achieve a balance was to make sure that Brooklyn Union had a leadership role going forward.

But as the Catacosinos controversy came to light, it became more difficult to convince people that the merger would proceed on a balanced, level playing field. Weinstein conducted meetings with her counterpart at LILCO along with his key team members. She remembers that in every meeting, no one but the LILCO HR director would speak. All the other team members would simply sit and observe the proceedings.

"Once the dollars are done, a merger is all about policy and practice," Weinstein recounted after the fact. "So when I first met with their director of HR, I saw this wonderfully talented HR executive who was smart, experienced, and deep within his discipline. But he'd spent his entire career at LILCO so he saluted to his leadership. It was apparent that he had marching orders.

"And I came in with my team, which was a very gregarious group. We like to talk, to have a good time, and we like to share. From that first day and for two months thereafter, the only person who spoke was their senior HR executive. He had at least 10 people with him. We met on neutral ground, and they sat behind him in a row. My people would talk to them but they would never answer. It was a bizarre experience.

"So when I had some quiet time with him, I said, 'This is crazy.

What is this about? These are obviously people you respect because you want them to hear everything. But they don't talk. Have you taken out their tongues?"

"And he said, 'That's just how we do things, Elaine.' I told him that this was simply not going to work here. It was terribly uncomfortable and embarrassing. He promised to speak to them and things picked up a little. But it was clear that Catacosinos had told him, 'You run the show.' "

As the two sides struggled to make sense of the situation, the pressure on the new board of directors to address the Catacosinos controversy took Catell's full attention. He and Craig Matthews tried to keep an emotional balance while seeking a way to work through the crisis. But it grew increasingly difficult to envision a way out of the abyss.

In late June, as the calamity began to reach a boiling point, Fred Lowther took Catell aside and made an outlandish suggestion. He advised Catell to go away, take a vacation, leave the center of the storm, and let Lowther and sympathetic board members work out a solution. "I knew this could get ugly," Lowther said. "I wanted Bob on safe ground, out of the line of fire and in a strong position once the dust settled."

For Catell, a man who has been known to leave on a "vacation" on a Saturday morning and return by Sunday night, the idea of leaving the scene was anathema. Yet he decided with great trepidation to follow Lowther's advice. He left, with more than a bit of irony, on a trip to Israel where biblical inspiration was available in abundance.

Meanwhile, it was obvious from reading the newspapers that the battle lines had been drawn. Governor Pataki, the LIPA administrators, and most of the politicians and regulators wanted Catacosinos out and Catell in. But Catacosinos dug in his heels and fought back. He had the backing of several large institutional shareholders who believed that Catacosinos was going to sell the new enterprise and maximize their investments.

For several weeks, the crisis took on the form of a civil war. Uncertainty about the eventual outcome took its toll. For Weinstein, the outcome at first seemed inevitable. "They were winning," she said about the LILCO executive team. So sure was she that Catacosinos would weather the storm and emerge victorious that she found another job and was ready to leave. She spoke to both Catell and Matthews and they convinced her to delay her decision. But resumes were flying out of Brooklyn Union like Hallmark cards on Mother's Day.

While Fred Lowther worked the legal issues, Ed Miller, a Brooklyn Union board member, headed up a special committee of the new board assigned to handle the crisis. As July progressed, it became apparent that the situation was reaching its climax. Catell, having returned from his hegira to the promised land, appeared on July 28 at a hearing of the New York State legislature. Under oath, he was able to describe publicly for the first time what had transpired with Catacosinos. His testimony described the nature of the transaction and when he was advised of the payout under the change of control provision. It was a critical turning point in a drama that would determine the leadership of the new corporation.

On that same day, the stock price of the new company dipped to under $26 a share, down sharply from $34 a share as recently as June 1. The new board understood that something had to be done to resolve the dispute. A special committee meeting and board meeting were called for that Friday, July 31. For Catell, his senior officers, and the entire population of the former Brooklyn Union, there was a surreal sense that everything was rushing to a final crescendo. It would be *High Noon*, and they had no idea who would be standing when the smoke finally cleared.

The CEO

~

When Fred Lowther suggested that I remove myself from the middle of the merger storm, I thought he was crazy. Since I became CEO of Brooklyn Union, I had been a reasonably public person, which makes it hard to go and hide in a corner. I'd been accessible to the press and I'd always felt comfortable being at the forefront of difficult business situations. But this time, I sensed that Fred was probably right, and though it would be extremely tough to leave, there might be some benefit to stepping out of the spotlight, at least for a while.

Clearly, I'd never experienced anything like this in my long career. I finally understood what the term "media frenzy" really meant. I was constantly getting late-night calls at home from the newspapers, and there was an endless series of requests during the day. The press realized that this was a big story and they were relentless. All the elements of a juicy controversy, with leading players like the governor, Catacosinos, and vocal politicians and regulators, made this irresistible.

But by July, I had reached a point where I needed a break. I had managed the press reasonably well by not saying anything and using the board of directors as my shield. Our lawyers advised me to be very careful about what I said and how I said it. This entire situation was growing increasingly litigious as events unfolded. The last thing I wanted to do was put the new company in a compromised position moving forward.

Over the past few months, I'd had little time to spend with Kenny and our employees. I'd already asked him to say a few extra prayers for me but I felt tremendous guilt and anxiety on behalf of my people. I knew how difficult this was for everyone. The uncertainty, the stigma associated with LILCO, and worst of all, the feeling that even though we had initiated the merger it was beginning to seem like a LILCO takeover, all combined to create a gloomy atmosphere.

Though I admit I had moments of doubt and pessimism, I was pretty good at keeping a smile on my face and presenting a positive front. I felt it was very important that I maintain the appropriate demeanor and that I show confidence that we would get through this and survive. But these were smart people and they understood that we had gone through the looking glass and, strange as things had become, we would need to follow events to their natural conclusion.

Needless to say, when I left for a trip to Israel in early July, I was anything but lighthearted and carefree. But it turned out to be a wonderful trip, much needed to relieve the pressure, but even more for its extraordinary spiritual impact. I'm not a particularly emotional person but this trip was an extremely emotional experience for me. Here, in this little corner of the world, where three great religions were born, so much has happened of significance. It helps put things into perspective. With my background in both Judaism and Catholicism, it felt in some ways like going home. I visited the synagogues, the churches, the mosques. I found myself praying a lot, not about the situation back home, but just to embrace the connection that one feels when visiting a place so sacred and awe-inspiring.

The group I was with made its way to Tiberias on the shores of the Sea of Galilee, a magical, beautiful place filled with meaning for me as a Catholic. This is the place where Jesus was supposed to have walked on water, and regardless of a person's beliefs, there is something miraculous and spiritual about visiting such a place. But before I could settle in, I received a phone message from one of the directors, Alan Fishman. I called him back in New York and he said, "Bob, are you aware that Bill Catacosinos has called a board meeting for this afternoon?" Of course, I knew nothing about it. "Well, I'm not sure what it's all about," Alan said, "but I understand he wants to discuss negotiating with another utility about buying the new company."

There I was, halfway around the world, hoping for a brief respite from the chaos at home and Act Two of this drama had begun without me. I suspected that this move in my absence was hardly a coincidence. In fact, I was starting to lose my patience with the good doctor.

Despite the huge time difference, I began making phone calls to my former Brooklyn Union directors to whom I was closest. I explained that this meeting was called without my knowledge. I had not been notified at all. I asked them to participate and make sure they were quite vocal during the proceedings.

There was certainly nothing illegal about calling a board meeting. Bill was the chairman and thus he had every right to call a board meeting. Under normal circumstances, however, the chairman would check in with the president and talk about the agenda. But it was obvious that there was another agenda at this point. If all this had been part of a bigger plan that he had harbored all along, it may have included plans to sell, or flip, the company and get another premium payout on top of the one he'd just received.

As a director, I should have been advised about the meeting well in advance. I tried to call Bill before the meeting. His secretary told me he was unavailable. She relayed his message that he would talk to me later at the meeting.

I sat in on the subsequent meeting by telephone. It lasted four hours. Bill discussed the possibility of soliciting an offer from the other utility. Numbers were tossed about, and the board, including me, asked a lot of questions. It wasn't particularly contentious given the circumstances. There was no yelling, just a very animated discussion. Ed Miller, Alan Fishman, and other former Brooklyn Union directors stepped to the plate and supported my position. It would not have been in the best interests of our shareholders to shop the company, particularly at a time when the stock was at a new low point.

This was the new board, which included six former LILCO directors. But they all proved their mettle that day and politely turned down Bill's proposal, pointing out that there was no reason at this particular time to enter into discussions and negotiations with another utility. Being professionals with a fiduciary responsibility to the shareholders, we kept the options open. But everyone—except Bill—

agreed that given all the uncertainty about the future of the company, the board, and particularly the CEO, it was not appropriate to initiate discussions about a new merger.

After I hung up the phone, I was relieved and upset and drained all at the same time. I had no hard evidence that Bill had planned something like this all along. It was only speculation on my part that from the very beginning he might have been waiting for the right opportunity to sell the company. By then, it was apparent to me that the situation was heading for a dramatic showdown. Whatever future Bill foresaw for MarketSpan certainly didn't line up with the future that I envisioned. I was trying to build a company and build value for our shareholders. Bill appeared to have another plan for the company's future. I knew two things: I hadn't brought Brooklyn Union this far in order to watch it get swept into oblivion in a series of mergers. And I no longer believed I could continue working with Bill for any significant period of time.

It was late. I had missed dinner that night with my traveling companions so I decided to take a walk down by the Sea of Galilee. I played the whole scenario out in my mind. In just a short time, everything I had envisioned seemed to be tumbling down. I wondered what I'd done wrong, and more important, how I could fix it. I knew that the stellar reputation that Brooklyn Union had built for over a hundred years was now at stake. A black cloud was hanging over this new company before we had even gotten started. Perception is often all that matters in situations like this, so I was very concerned about our employees and the future.

I am not a confrontational person. My style is to be more conciliatory, though I had never experienced anything like this in my 40-year career. I was furious with Bill, and absolutely outraged at both what he was doing and how he was doing it. But I needed to channel my rage in a more constructive direction. There was no point in trying to discuss this with him any further. I had tried to reach out to him when the situation first came to light. I said, "You know, you really don't have to do this. If you're entitled to a retirement package, you'll get it when you retire." He didn't want to hear any of that.

So as I walked along the Sea of Galilee, I prayed quietly. I said a prayer of thanks and asked for the strength to keep moving forward while we worked out the solution to this crisis. I was heading home in a couple of days so there was no need to rush for the next plane. No doubt events would start moving more quickly as July came to a close. The board had established a special committee that was investigating the Catacosinos package. I had a clear sense that the committee would do the right thing from a corporate standpoint. They were under a lot of pressure. The governor was calling for Bill to resign. There were vocal shareholders threatening lawsuits, some of which eventually were filed. And in the space of a few short months, a promising journey had veered wildly off course.

When I returned to Brooklyn, the board called an emergency meeting for July 31. We convened in the law offices of Simpson Thacher in Manhattan in order to avoid the press, which was clamoring to find out what would transpire at the meeting. No sooner had the group settled in around the conference table than Ed Miller, chairman of the special committee, requested an executive session and asked both Bill and me to leave the room. Though I'd suspected this would happen, I hadn't known for sure. Obviously it was high noon and some very hard decisions were about to be made.

Incredibly, Bill and I were asked to wait together in a separate conference room down the hall. Talk about an awkward moment. I hadn't spoken to Bill since the phone meeting in Israel. Suddenly, there we were sitting in a room looking at each other, knowing that our fates were being decided a few steps away in that meeting. We tried to make small talk—"How's your wife?" "Fine. And yours?"—but the time for that had obviously passed. The tension was thick; you could cut the air with the proverbial knife. We both knew one of us wasn't going to survive at the new company. I have no idea what was going through his mind. Being the kind of person he is, I suspect he believed he'd be asked to stay on.

It had become apparent to me by then that I was someone who was essentially in the way of his plans. The mutual respect I thought we'd achieved had been one-sided. He wasn't smug. That wasn't his style. He was fairly cold and aloof. Mostly, we sat in uncomfortable silence for the longest half hour I'd ever spent. I finally couldn't take it anymore and went out to make a phone call. By the time I returned, he'd been called into the board meeting.

So I sat by myself for another 45 minutes. I heard no shouting or angry words from down the hall. I was later told that the board had explained their disappointment and concern about what had transpired. They told him they had the perception that he had been aggressively looking to push me to the side and they were determined to make sure that didn't happen. And then they'd asked for his resignation.

Bill didn't display any anger. He was apparently disappointed, having thought he'd get enough support from the former LILCO board members to prevail. He left quietly out another door.

The board then called me in. I didn't see Bill leave. I was told that Bill had resigned and that I was going to be the new chairman and CEO of the company. And then the board members applauded. It was a very sweet sound, let me tell you. It was an extremely emotional moment for me, perhaps the milestone moment of my career. I thanked the directors for their support and told them that I was committed to moving the company forward. They all expressed a great deal of confidence in my ability to do that, and it felt great.

When we left the law offices, the press was waiting outside en masse. They had found out our location and the frenzy began. I had to be almost lifted bodily through the crowd of reporters and television cameras. They were literally grabbing my clothes, demanding an interview. I thought, "This is what it must feel like to be a rock star." I was not prepared for that and was happy to be whisked into a waiting limousine. I had promised that we would have a press release and a press conference later in the afternoon, which we did.

And as I sat back in that limo, I had a moment to think that sometimes, the right thing does happen. It was a perfect moment. And when it passed, the next thing I thought was, we're going to rename this company KeySpan.

The Monk

*W*hen I was in the monastery, my spiritual director, Father Theodore, would occasionally talk to me about "the dark night of the soul." It was a term used by the monks of old to describe the shadow side of an individual's pursuit of personal holiness. This was a period of time marked by self-recrimination, discouragement, and a lack of hope. This arid wasteland of spiritual depression could last for weeks or sometimes months and was an inevitable part of one's interior journey. "Your faith will be tested and you will feel lost and abandoned," was the way he put it.

Religious life is not the sole domain of this Dante-like journey into the depths of darkness. It happens in our personal lives as well. The loss of employment or the breakup of an intimate relationship can cause the same malaise. I encountered the dark night of the soul in my yearlong bout with cancer. Bob was meeting his as the merger unfolded.

There's no simple cure for this listlessness of the spirit. It needs to be experienced, endured, and traveled through. If all goes well, you come out of it a deeper person. If not, you can lose your faith and spend many years in bitter resentment.

There is no sure way of guaranteeing success at the outset, but many sacred traditions offer sound advice for navigating this trying experience. While there was not much business wisdom I could offer Bob regarding the merger, I did take advantage of one of my few meetings with him to offer support and share what little spiritual wisdom I had.

"When all hell breaks loose, it helps to stay focused on the ordinary and the simple," I advised. "Hold on to normal routines, keep moving forward, and try not to lose hope." We both understood that at this vulnerable time it was even more important for him to reach out to trusted allies for assistance, which was something well underway.

I reminded him of the words of Elisabeth Kübler-Ross: "People are like stained-glass windows. They sparkle and shine when the sun is out, but when the darkness sets in, their beauty is revealed only if there is a light from within." What ultimately saves us from personal destruction during this lonely journey is the depth of our interior life. It is less a question of physical strength and more an issue of individual character. The tools for this engagement are reflection, prayer, and the mustering of all one's spiritual resources.

While Bob was busy waging an outside battle in the corporate world, I encouraged him to strengthen his interior resolve as well. "Don't lose your soul in the midst of this drama. Make sure you find a personal space for yourself and your God in this whirlwind of activity."

In ancient times, people would make pilgrimages to sacred sites seeking divine assistance in times of distress. When the spiritual journey proved desolate, making a physical one often wound up being redemptive. I remember calling Bob to schedule another brief meeting only to be told that he was away from the office. Away? In the midst of a crisis? It struck me as odd.

"Where did he go?" I asked his secretary. "He's on vacation over in Israel," she replied. I thought to myself: That's not a vacation, that's a pilgrimage. His instincts were good and I wondered what spiritual enlightenment awaited him in the Holy Land. In my heart, I wished him well and took a walk down to the Cathedral of St. James to light a candle for his personal intentions. I likewise lit a votive light for the company as well.

In times of crisis, it is best to offer hope, not request it. For my own part, I also privately met with executives in Brooklyn to offer support and bolster confidence. As one of our executives told me: "We don't need your help in setting our goals. What we need from you now is a miracle. Now get to work on it!" As savvy executives, they were also hosting private meetings on their own and surreptitiously brokering alternate strategies.

As the scandal broke in the news, the company also descended into its own dark night of the soul. Many employees from both Brooklyn and Long Island were personally upset and emotionally torn. Just as there are no answers when making one's personal journey within this darkness, there is likewise no corporate road map for success, either. One would need to be crafted as we moved forward.

For the employees in Brooklyn, the new organizational chart revealed a dominance of LILCO officers in key positions. Some framed this outcome in a "win-lose" scenario, with LILCO having the organizational upper hand and Brooklyn Union officers coming in a distant second. They felt that their worst fears had been realized and that a command-and-control management style would pervade the new corporate culture. While some spoke of passive submission and others of open revolution, many updated their resumes, feeling compelled to seek employment elsewhere.

While in my heart I shared their concerns, I didn't feel the need to update my own resume. After you've come close to dying from cancer, the prospect of losing your job doesn't really strike fear into your soul. Part of me even approached all these corporate machinations with a sense of gallows humor. The most they could do would be to fire me, not kill me. Keeping this perspective in mind, I was able to carry on with a sense of patience and hopeful expectation.

In my dealings with employees I tried to maintain an atmosphere of calm and nonreactionary behavior. We didn't need groups of lemming-like employees committing political suicide or becoming corporate martyrs for a worthy cause. My years of studying church history made me familiar with the consequence of such actions. Martyrdom gets you a dramatic moment before the crowd but your ability to influence future outcomes is all but eliminated. I was looking for responses that were more sustainable and rested on a solid middle ground.

One of the things I learned in the cancer ward is that there are no quick fixes to our problems, no miracles that suddenly appear to remedy a bad situation. You have to show up day after day, go through some uncomfortable experiences . . . and pray. I also knew that it helps to not feel alone during these rough periods. Staying isolated weakens the soul and depletes the mind. So I sought to find ways of bringing people together for both social and business reasons.

For the employees working with me in the human resources department, I started hosting regular birthday celebrations. Every month we'd gather in a conference room over coffee and cookies to sing "Happy Birthday" to co-workers, update each other on organizational changes, as well as share recent corporate events. Sometimes I'd get one of our executives to stop by and offer moral support to the group. Soon, other departments were also having these kinds of gatherings.

I would also bring along my astrology book and read horoscopes, trying to interpret the stars and predict the future. It was mostly futile, and uproariously insane and funny. G. K. Chesterton said that hope is the power of being cheerful in circumstances that we know to be desperate. These informal celebrations were an opportunity to spend playful time with co-workers, release some anxious energy, and help build community in our small part of the organizational world.

I also spent a good part of my time supporting and counseling individual employees. Some of these conversations took place in my office. Others were held in coffee shops far removed from company locations. There were times I felt like Henry Kissinger, performing shuttle diplomacy to keep interested parties involved in the future of the business. I did this all in the hope that, with the passage of time, some creative spark might ignite a workable solution.

I often encountered employees who were able to draw from the wealth of their personal experiences to make sense of a difficult situation. As one employee told me over drinks in a back-room bar in the bowels of Brooklyn, "If I could survive my divorce, I can certainly survive this ordeal."

In unique ways, many workers were able to bring their life skills to the fore in meeting the challenges confronting the company. "I was one of five kids when my mom died," an engineer told me. "Dad quickly remarried, and his new wife was a widow with four kids of her own. In a matter of a few short months we had two separate families living in the same big house. It was both crazy and challenging." She knew something about stepfamilies and how to build alliances with new members of the family, whether personal or corporate. "It all looks familiar to me, and I think I might be able to help the merger work out."

For the employees from Long Island, many were distressed about the uproar. They had hoped that retiring the LILCO name would remove them from the harsh light of the media and provide a clean start with a new company image. As one employee told me: "Just when we get a chance to clear our name and start anew, we're right back in the negative spotlight."

In early June, I was invited to be one of the speakers at the first meeting of all the officers of the merged company. The room looked like a family gathering of the Hatfields and McCoys, with each group solidly positioned in their respective corners. They might as well have been wearing Yankees and Red Sox uniforms. Each stayed to themselves and mingling was at a minimum. The gathering appeared as an odd array of personalities and egos trying to find their places in a new corporate setting. Many of the executives from Long Island seemed somewhat humorless and took themselves and the business at hand with overbearing seriousness.

I introduced myself by explaining the type of work I did for the company. The eyes of the LILCO officers rolled in bemusement. I then went on to share with them the feedback from my many meetings with employees during the past few months.

"Employees are longing for more involvement and empowerment. They have much to offer and feel excluded from the process," I said to a room growing colder from stares by the Long Island officers. "Many employees fear that the officer team won't work well together. A few believe that there's not even a desire on your part to make it work." I then went on and offered some recommendations for empowering employees and enhancing the officers' stature within the new company.

Every new venture deserves a patron saint. I decided the poet Walt Whitman would be the perfect patron saint of this journey. He was born on Long Island yet worked much of his life in Brooklyn. He was likewise an advocate for the common laborer and a man of community service. And lastly, not only was Whitman an exemplary poet, he was also an astute businessman. When requests for his book *Leaves of Grass* dwindled, he took to the streets and aggressively used the media to improve sales. He sounded like a worthy model for the new group, and I offered him as such.

Alas, my comments were met with little warmth from the LILCO side of the room. For many of them, business and humor did not mix. Employee feedback was seen as irrelevant to the running of the business. While the Brooklyn Union officers did not always agree with my style, they always supported the underlying intent of my work. There was a marked dichotomy within the room that day.

I learned later that after I had left the room, one of the LILCO officers loudly announced, "Well, there's one opportunity to reduce head count that won't negatively impact the business." For me, that was a sobering glimpse of my possible future within the new organization.

During that summer right after the merger, there was also much work to be done with the larger employee community. When corporate unrest permeates the workplace, employees can feel like helpless victims. This can destroy the soul of an organization and wreak havoc on corporate performance. It's helpful at times like this to bring employees together and pin their attention on things they understand and can control. The focus needs to be practical and tangible. Bob had often counseled me during the merger process: "No matter what happens, I want you to keep working for the good of the company. Your commitment needs to be to the corporation, not an individual. Don't forget that."

I kept those words in mind even though corporate life had become a bit strained. I reached out to broker relationships with officers from Long Island to continue the Employee Care meetings. Prior to the merger, these sessions remained small and focused on capturing employee input. Now that the merger was complete, I wanted them to include larger numbers of employees and be directly connected to pressing business needs.

With the merger moving into full implementation, new organizations were in place and people from both companies were joined into singular departments. The practical task of running a day-to-day operation proved to be a healthy distraction from some of the corporate friction surrounding us.

Even under the shadow of controversy surrounding the Catacosinos payment, the business of the business continued. I worked in bringing together large groups of employees from both Brooklyn and Long Island and focusing their attention on meeting business goals. Operations had to be integrated. Customers needed to be satisfied. Sales had to be made. I repeatedly witnessed large groups of employees getting beyond their myopic self-interest and contributing to the overall success of the company.

By patiently hammering away, I began to win converts on Long Island. A new style of Employee Care meetings began, this time focused on practical business issues rather than simply on getting employee feedback. Each session resulted in a detailed list of action items to improve division performance. While some remained skeptical of my approach, many agreed with the end result. As utility executives they understood that regardless of who won the political battle at the top of the house, business success took precedence.

To the degree they experienced me as supporting that overarching goal, I gained credibility in their eyes. As one Long Island officer told me privately: "I initially thought you were all fluff and had no business sense at all. Now I'm beginning to see some of the value of the work you do."

As I was leaving this uplifting conversation, I received the news that Bob had been elected CEO by the board. Now was the time for refocusing energy, mending corporate fractures, and moving the company forward to benefit from the assets of the merger. I also hoped that the dark night of the soul had passed and we would grow wiser as individuals and a corporation from the experience.

Incidentally, when the first annual report of the merged company was published several months later, it contained a quote from Walt Whitman. Our patron saint had watched over us and I experienced it as a small triumph for my heart.

CHAPTER SIX

~

The Aftermath

He who wishes to secure the good of others, has already secured his own.

—Confucius

Sometimes, as the old saying goes, you have to be careful what you ask for because you just might get it. Having emerged victorious in the showdown with Catacosinos, Bob Catell's future became markedly more complicated. He now faced the daunting proposition of pulling the staggered merger back on track and getting both sides over the shell shock of what had transpired.

Catell's emergence as chairman was widely acclaimed. An editorial in the *Brooklyn Daily Eagle* proclaimed: "We Believe in Robert Catell." The paper trumpeted Catell's leadership and the company's excellent track record as a community-oriented organization that gave its customers the best possible services at the most reasonable rates. "We hold to our belief that Robert Catell, who always could be counted on to work for the best interests of Brooklyn, will be just as great an asset to the people of all of Long Island," the paper predicted.

The kudos notwithstanding, Catell knew that the aftermath was going to be protracted and difficult. Beyond the usual merger trauma for both companies, the events of the summer had turned the process into a nightmare. In fact, the summer of 1998 quickly became labeled "the dark period" for employees in both premerger companies.

As bad as it had been for Brooklyn Union's leadership, it was equally painful for the rank and file. Tensions were high, and employees, on call and under the gun for sustained periods during the summer, sought various ways to deal with a situation they could not influence, let alone control. Not surprisingly, some were spiritually inspired. Nondenominational early-morning prayer meetings were held outside business hours, for employees of all faiths. There were prayer groups and prayer chains, all seemingly aimed at winning divine intervention in Catell's favor. But while such activities helped, the summer had left a trail of painful memories, and corporate post-traumatic stress syndrome set in.

Kenny Moore didn't participate in the prayer meetings. Though he knew people appreciated his religious background and training, he was no longer an ordained officiate, and he firmly believed that his role should respect secular boundaries. Besides, he had his hands full trying to establish lines of communication between the merged entities. He felt that Catell's emergence had a spiritual quality to it, a kind of redemption that would be felt keenly by the Brooklyn Unionites but would be embraced far less out on Long Island. Crossing such a chasm would require great strength, patience, and insight, traits he would call upon from his monastic life. He would also draw heavily on Catell himself as a crucial source of inspiration. Moore already knew what type of person Catell was, but now he would witness the grace under pressure that would become Catell's trademark throughout the coming months.

One of Catell's strengths as a leader had been an ability to move ahead and not dwell on the past. It would be easy to sit back and analyze the past few months, but he had no interest in that. In fact, the afternoon he walked out of the law offices in Manhattan as the new company's CEO, Catell got on the phone and began calling the union leadership to assure the unions from both companies that there would be no layoffs as the new company moved ahead. Ralph Ranghelli, the head of the electrical workers union on Long Island, was impressed that minutes after being named CEO, Catell called him personally. It is a story he continues to tell when citing his admiration for Catell.

The next day, Catell went out to LILCO's Hicksville headquarters to meet with employees and welcome them into the new company. He told them they would all be treated fairly and honestly as part of the new company. He also assured them there would be no layoffs due to the merger and urged them to keep an open mind about the future. Though it would take a long time to meld corporate cultures, the former LILCO employees got their first exposure to Catell and saw the stark contrast between his style and Catacosinos'.

For most of them, there was a certain level of disbelief. Many thought such an affable, accessible persona must be a put-on, too good to be true. Catell's personality aside, the biggest fear for the employees of LILCO's vast electric business was that their futures were tenuous because Brooklyn Union was, at heart, a gas company and the gas side would rule.

That same afternoon, Catell arrived at MetroTech headquarters for a meeting with the former Brooklyn Union employees. As he entered the packed auditorium, filled to capacity with more than 400 people, he received a thunderous standing ovation. After months of anticipating a worst-case scenario—working for Catacosinos in a LILCO-dominated setting—the Brooklyn Union people had been thrilled to see Catell's triumph. Sometimes, truth and justice *did* prevail.

No one, according to Elaine Weinstein, was as surprised as the Brooklyn Union executive team. It was like the Brooklyn Dodgers finally beating the Yankees in the 1955 World Series. The resulting euphoria was mixed with a renewed respect and just a bit of awe of Catell. "Here was this very humble, affable, charming guy, and it turned out he was very shrewd and very political," Weinstein says. "He is someone who knows how to play the game incredibly well."

It had nothing to do with Catell maneuvering or scheming to oust Catacosinos. It was based entirely on a long career's worth of integrity coupled with building and sustaining the right connections in Albany and throughout the industry. Reputations, it turned out, do matter.

Good will was a potent force. The utilities business is highly political, and Catell, by sticking to his core values, managed to turn the politics in his favor. "Bob has chosen a life of public service through this company," Weinstein explains. "He has given himself totally, and he's done the right thing. He's delivered for this city and this community. And there are some paybacks."

The very deliberate resolve that ensured his victory gave Catell confidence that he could rescue this merger. But before Catell could even begin to find a way to bridge the two camps, he had to settle one more significant issue: what to do about the 26 LILCO executives and their $25 million worth of golden parachutes that had been part of the Catacosinos controversy. While the payments were nowhere near the Catacosinos level, each officer had received anywhere from $700,000 to $4 million. The early perception was that the LILCO officers would not only get these lucrative payouts but get to keep their jobs in the new company as well. Needless to say, this set off sparks throughout the new organization.

It was obvious that the legality of the payouts was now beyond question. If Catacosinos' package was technically legal, so were those of the LILCO officers. But Catell knew immediately that allowing all the significant LILCO executives to keep both the money and their jobs would create two classes of KeySpan officers. And that was simply not going to fly.

Catell did not take long to formulate a solution. Within a couple of days, he sent word to the LILCO officers that they had to make a choice: stay with the new company and return the money or leave.

He had begun deliberating as to which officers of the 26 he wanted to retain. He'd identified 14 who he hoped would be willing to return the money. In the chess game of moving executives into positions within a merged entity, the political and emotional fallout was always intense. No matter how you couched it, there were winners and losers. Employees from both sides watched closely to see how the pieces would land and how it would impact their jobs and lives.

Catell had to find a delicate balance: keeping enough Brooklyn Union officers in place to be representative of the former company but not alienate the LILCO population by underrepresenting their side. His own colleagues worried that Catell would be trying so hard to ingratiate himself with the LILCO people that he would overcompensate and give them the best positions. The LILCO executives, especially on the electric side, assumed they were soon to become second-class citizens.

The process bogged down in the first few weeks after Catacosinos departed. The LILCO officers had to choose between their jobs and their payouts, and many dragged their feet. Tony Nozzolillo, LILCO's chief financial officer and senior vice president, was among those in a quandary. They didn't believe they were acting with greed, Nozzolillo says. They had long believed themselves underpaid based on industry averages and benchmarks of other companies. They also believed the payouts were completely legal, and many had convinced themselves they could keep both the money and their jobs.

"Once you give out the money and then ask for it back, that's a totally different world," Nozzolillo explains. "It's different than if they never saw the money at all. And I don't recall any discussions about the morality of the payouts. Nobody asked, 'Is this the moral thing to do?' This was business; it was part of the deal."

For many, the decision was easy. They simply could not comprehend returning such sums and figured, in the robust economy of the late 1990s, they would find new jobs quickly. A few thought about it longer.

The Brooklyn Union officers waited amid some tension and bitterness for the decisions to be made. "We were sitting there waiting to find out who would be following Catacosinos out the door," recalls Bob Fani. "We wondered who would be the first to step up and say, 'I'm committed to the new KeySpan. Here's my money back.' The only way we were going to become a team is if we all felt we were playing for the same team in exactly the same way."

Eventually, 19 of the 26 officers chose to keep their windfalls and depart. Of the seven who chose to remain, Nozzolillo was the only senior LILCO officer. He returned his payment. For Nozzolillo, the decision was based on impending retirement, not far off on the horizon.

He was just three or four years from being able to exercise his pension and wanted the flexibility to retire when he was ready. He'd also spent a lot of time with Bob Catell and Craig Matthews and believed that they honestly wanted him to stay and that he had a real future with the company. There was another, more compelling reason: "From day one, my wife felt that it was not my money," he says, laughing.

Making the decision more palatable, Nozzolillo and the other LILCO officers who chose to stay were given stock options that could eventually equal or surpass the amount they had returned, assuming the company's performance provided a bright future. Today, Nozzolillo is executive vice president in charge of KeySpan's entire electric business on Long Island. His blue-collar Brooklyn background and affable personality made him a perfect fit with his new colleagues. "I'm a people person," he says. "I felt comfortable working with Bob Catell, and I never felt like an outsider. I always looked upon this as a new entity, not as Brooklyn Union or LILCO."

The departure of so many LILCO officers, however, shifted the balance at the top of the new company heavily toward the former Brooklyn Union. On Long Island, despite Catell's entreaties to be patient and open-minded about the new organization, the perception was widespread that this had become a Brooklyn Union takeover and that the LILCO era had come to an end. People were worried about the future, and only time and keeping to a consistent message would begin to change attitudes.

Over time, the LILCO people softened. At Moore's behest, Catell made frequent visits with his new employees. He set up a second headquarters in Hicksville and spent a significant amount of time there. The face-to-face meetings eventually wore down the cynicism among the majority of the workers. They particularly appreciated Catell's efforts to show personal interest in the electric business. He was forthcoming, acknowledging his lack of knowledge of their world but making it clear that he was ready to learn. He also pointed out that managing the electric business owned by LIPA with its $2.5 billion in revenues provided opportunities for KeySpan to become a larger electric generation company, a key reason he had sought the merger in the first place. He most certainly wanted it to thrive and grow.

And more than at any other time in their partnership, Moore's presence in the center of the storm provided a crucial conduit to Long Island. LILCO had once tried to install its own corporate ombudsman but its internal atmosphere was so contentious that the position proved ineffective. Moore began an earnest attempt to bring the new entity together, working with both sides of the new organization to open lines of communication.

Nozzolillo says that Moore brought a peace of mind to many people on Long Island; he presented the human side of the company in a way that calmed people's fears. "He plays a critical role in my organization," Nozzolillo says. "Everybody loves him. He earns his respect and has an incredible sense of humor. I have truly never heard one person say they disliked or mistrusted Kenny.

"He's sincere. He understands cultural differences. He participates and tells you what he feels, and he's a phenomenal listener," Nozzolillo continues. "You can pour your soul out to him and because we know his background, a lot of us Christians feel very close to that. There's a sense of respect knowing he was a priest. Mostly, he is a man of action. He tries to resolve things."

As with any large-scale corporate merger, the LILCO deal has moved forward in fits and starts. Over time, the sharp edges have been worn down by the sustained efforts of the CEO and the monk, as well as a committed cadre of old and new officers. The majority of former LILCO employees have become proud and enthusiastic KeySpan employees and have embraced its culture and community commitment.

Not only did the merger allow for immediate electricity rate decreases, but KeySpan made significant efforts to quickly establish its strong community-oriented presence on Long Island. Sponsoring such critical campaigns as promoting awareness of breast cancer, a particularly troubling disease on Long Island, along with spreading its corporate charity to other local causes and institutions, KeySpan emerged as the antithesis to LILCO. Working for a company that had a soul and the means to support that soul provided a dramatic contrast for employees who had labored for decades under austerity budgets and ceaseless financial woes.

As the new millennium approached, Catell felt energized and optimistic. By the end of 2000, Wall Street had reacted positively to the merger. With Enron flexing its vaunted muscle, the energy sector looked ripe for a massive makeover. But KeySpan had solid underpinnings, lots of cash, and strong leadership in place. It might make an attractive takeover target, or it might just surprise some people and emerge as a player.

In September, 1998, shortly after the merger had been consummated, KeySpan sponsored an employee appreciation day at Shea Stadium. More than 7,000 employees and their families, wearing KeySpan T-shirts, came out to celebrate at a New York Mets game. In a short ceremony before the game, Bob Catell stood out on the field shoulder to shoulder with some of the Mets players and watched as Thomas Russo, a union worker from LILCO, threw out the first pitch. Catell had invited Russo as a way of reaching out to the former LILCO side with a gesture that was deeply meaningful to him personally. Amid the loudest cheers he had ever heard, Catell thought back to his childhood dreams of one day standing on a major league baseball diamond. As Russo reared back and grooved a fastball over the plate, Catell beamed, with a grin that seemed to stretch from Brooklyn all the way to the tip of Long Island.

The CEO

~

In the six months following the LILCO merger, I was probably as stressed as I had ever been in my entire career. The emotional roller coaster I had been on personally seemed to run parallel to that of the company itself. Everyone was anxious and frazzled to the breaking point. It was difficult to observe this company that was so much a part of me struggling to find itself in this turbulent time. In some ways, it was harder to witness the former LILCO people. I didn't know them. I hadn't hired them and grown up alongside them. Yet I now felt very responsible for them and for finding a way to bring them into the fold. I knew I had my work cut out for me. It was going to take more than ball games at Shea.

Kenny was working overtime to build some important bridges. He began leading sessions with managers from both organizations in hopes of opening a dialogue that would bridge a wide gap between cultures. He would later explain to me how uplifting it felt to observe the LILCO managers in what, for them, was such an unfamiliar atmosphere, an atmosphere of open communication and mutual respect from the top levels of the company.

Not long after the merger, for example, Kenny organized a leadership meeting with 500 executives and managers from both sides of the new company. In his ombudsman role, he had been hearing how difficult it was for people to feel comfortable with the new environment. Former Brooklyn Union people said that it didn't feel like it was their company anymore. So here was a chance to get the movers and shakers into a room together to confront some of these feelings of alienation.

After the executive vice presidents spoke about their business plans and took some questions, I got up to introduce the second part of the meeting. I explained that I had seen more change in the industry in the past two years than at any time before. "And more is coming," I warned. I pointed out that instead of reading *Oil & Gas Journal*, I was now reading magazines like *Fast Company*. Change doesn't necessarily request an invitation; it often just shows up unannounced and uninvited. We had to be ready for that, comfortable or not.

"And now for something completely different," I said, quoting *Monty Python* as I introduced Kenny. He explained how he felt, which undoubtedly resonated with the audience. "I have all these answers," he said, "but people aren't asking me the right questions." He echoed my thoughts about how fast the world was changing and how difficult it is to prepare for that. He then introduced a "corporate comic" named Izzy Gesell, which caused a buzz to ripple through the room. Izzy specialized in the art of improvisational comedy, or improv. He often worked with large organizations like NASA, IBM, and the Internal Revenue Service on facing and responding to change. Even for the former Brooklyn Union folks, already used to Kenny's sometimes wild ideas, this was a bit quirky. For the LILCO people, it bordered on the outlandish. Needless to say, there hadn't been much comedy on Long Island. It certainly grabbed everyone's attention.

Izzy was funny. "I enjoy my neuroses," he explained. "They've been with me a long time." He then explained the concept of improv. Comedians study and practice improv, which is both a discipline and an art form. It requires a person to react spontaneously and immediately with a willingness to forge ahead and leave the constrictions of preparation and planning behind. In a world changing this fast, corporations like KeySpan had to be ready to forgo the traditional ways of pondering and researching every move. We had to be able to move forward quickly, improvising and performing the best we could under the circumstances that the marketplace handed us.

While we were building this new organization amid the swirling changes in the energy industry, we would indeed have to improvise on the fly. We had a great group of talented people, but what we lacked was the playfulness, the spontaneity, the willingness to accommodate mistakes and move the agenda forward.

Izzy asked for volunteers. Everyone looked away, not wanting to be chosen. He prodded us and asked us how we could hope to lead our troops if we were not willing to take risks. One brave manager stepped onto the stage and gave it a try. Everyone relaxed. It was fascinating to watch how quickly people switched from avoiding Izzy's gaze in hopes of not being chosen to waving their hands to participate. Laughter filled the room. Eventually, one of the union leaders yelled out, "Why aren't the executives playing?" Good question. I immediately volunteered along with some of the senior officers. I was supposed to provide the last line of a spontaneously created limerick, and I flubbed it badly. We tried again, and I did better the next time. Kenny later congratulated me for sending the message that it was okay to make mistakes as long as you were willing to be part of the process. If the chairman is up there, it ripples through the community that change is coming; we may not handle it perfectly, but we will always be better off finding new ways to embrace the future.

The good thing about Kenny's meetings was that people generally exited feeling better than when they arrived. Like missionaries, they would take the message they had heard back out to their people. But now we had 8,000 employees, and reaching all of them was going to take time. We brought in stress counselors to help people cope. I remembered how we had done the corporate funeral years before as a way to help people deal with change when we felt the first waves of deregulation coming our way. Now, that seemed like child's play compared to this. This was going to require more than a single symbolic gesture.

What was very apparent, almost as soon as the board handed me the keys to KeySpan's CEO suite, was that bringing together these two very different, very unique companies was going to require some deep sensitivity and proactive thinking on my part. After all was said and done, what we needed was nothing less than a completely new culture! Though I believed deeply in the Brooklyn Union way, I realized that it would never work to simply layer what we were on top of the new entity and hope for the best. We had to create a new set of corporate values and a new mission statement, and work toward building a culture that incorporated the best of both companies.

Here we had this large electric division from LILCO and we had never been in the electrical business before. They felt they had to convince us that the electrical business was important to us. And despite its public relations difficulties, LILCO brought extensive levels of excellence to the table. Though it had obviously failed to overcome its unfavorable status out in the community, LILCO was a state-of-the-art company operationally. There was much we could learn from what they had accomplished, especially given that so much had to be done under the most difficult circumstances.

So I knew that my new senior team and I would be spending a lot of time on Long Island, meeting with employees, getting the officers to talk, creating this new set of values. In the end, the new values statement was different from those of Brooklyn Union and LILCO. For KeySpan, we incorporated a core set of beliefs: honesty, integrity, diversity, and community involvement. Certainly much of this had long been part of the Brooklyn Union psyche, but in the new entity, I had to make sure that the officers would walk the talk and that this was really a model we would be measured against.

I could tell early on that being measured this way by these new standards was very foreign to the LILCO people, obviously less so for the Brooklyn Union side. The LILCO employees had always been evaluated based strictly on job performance and achievements, usually tied to financial targets. For me, this was only part of the equation. I've always believed that a business can be humanistic, and with that model, I believe you can integrate personal values in how a company runs and still keep it in the top quartile of performance.

KeySpan was going to focus far more on the corporate values and tie that into salary and incentives payouts. What meaning do you bring to the company? Do you practice the corporate values? For example, do you believe in diversity, do you demonstrate that you can motivate people, do you treat people with dignity and respect? Are you active in the community?

Part of my very practical problem was replacing the cadre of officers who had headed for the exits with their golden parachutes. I had met with each of the 26 LILCO officers individually to discuss the situation. There was no belligerence or resentment. On the contrary, each was very gracious and thoughtful about the dilemma. Most simply could not justify returning such a large sum of money and were more comfortable leaving for destinations unknown. A few stressed to me that they were legally entitled to the money. I had to explain to them that though that was an appropriate legal interpretation, they simply couldn't put themselves in a different place than the other KeySpan officers.

As it became obvious that most were leaving, I had to sit down and create a new executive team. This meant leaning on my Brooklyn Union team initially but finding ways to promote deserving LILCO managers who had been waiting in the wings for an opportunity.

As that was unfolding, we began the process of changing our image on Long Island. We began a full-court press to create a presence in the community as we had done for 100 years in Brooklyn. Our employees have always been encouraged and supported to get out and get involved in every kind of community effort, from walks for hunger to teaching at adult education programs, to sitting on local boards for Junior Achievement. Volunteerism had, over time, become part of the fabric of the company, the foundation for our embrace of enlightened self-interest.

In addition to our corporate giving, the presence of KeySpan employees out in the community began, relatively quickly, to make an impact on Long Island. We are not shy about letting it be known that supporting community groups is part of the corporate ethic. We'll even pay employee expenses and try to provide flexibility in their schedules. This is, after all, our community, too, and this time and effort is an investment that pays for itself many times over. We started hearing from citizen groups about how refreshing it was to have a company out there that cares about the community. We wanted the KeySpan logo to invoke feelings of goodwill, and in a surprisingly short time, it has done just that. As in Brooklyn, Staten Island, and

Queens, we have put a face on the company on Long Island, as executives and employees spend a tremendous amount of time and energy doing volunteer work in the community.

At the same time, we made mistakes. We took the KeySpan name for the holding company and decided that we should use the Brooklyn Union name for our gas operations, including on Long Island. Truthfully, I was hesitant to abandon the Brooklyn Union name. The brand equity from a 103-year-old institution with decades' worth of positive connection to the community was tough to discard. But we quickly realized that having different names for different parts of the business was simply confusing the customers. So we united under the name KeySpan for the length and breadth of the company. That meant removing the Brooklyn Union name altogether, even in Brooklyn, Queens, and Staten Island. This decision, while necessary, has always troubled me. Even years later, I still occasionally get razzed by people in Brooklyn for abandoning a much beloved name. But sometimes, as Kenny reminds me, you have to let go of the past before you can discover the future.

At the same time, we had promised as part of the merger that we would reduce our costs by $100 million per year for 10 years. That, of course, meant reducing our head count, which was not an optimum situation while trying to bridge cultures and build trust. We were able to meet our initial goals with early retirement packages and thus avoid layoffs, as I had promised. I know that some former Brooklyn Union folks think we lost a few too many good people from our side during this period. Whether or not that was true, we had to move forward with the players we had. We also had to start eliminating the "us versus them" feeling that inevitably infects postmerger companies.

But there was more. All through this period, as tough as things got, I had to remain focused and upbeat. As the new CEO, I had to represent a confident new organization to the industry, the financial community, the politicians, and the employees. I realized that I had to meet and ingratiate myself with a whole new cadre of elected officials on Long Island. The reality of a regulated business is that no matter how much good you do, you need to work the system, understand the various agendas, and find ways to cross into many camps with your stakeholders' message.

Not a small amount of my time was taken up with the financial community and the perceptions of the marketplace. Remember that this was the time when Enron was gaining momentum and sending out a message that companies like KeySpan were dinosaurs, soon to be extinct when Enron fulfilled its destiny. We were getting steady pressure from Wall Street and large institutional investors to change, to become more like Enron, to get into the energy trading business. Financial types with concepts and ideas kept calling, wanting to build trading operations for us or form alliances. I resisted it all, but warily.

And deregulation hadn't disappeared. The Public Service Commission ordered the electric utilities to sell their generation plants. Con Edison had to put its electricity generating plants up for sale, and we made a successful bid for its giant Ravenswood plant. We had emerged from the LILCO deal with significant cash, and this seemed like too good an opportunity to pass up. Ravenswood supplied 25 percent of the power that lit up New York City. It was a valuable asset. We paid $600 million for the plant, and it turned out to be an excellent investment. But coming in the midst of Enron's new "paradigm," which claimed that companies shouldn't own any assets, it was yet another reminder to Wall Street that we were not following Enron's lead.

I admit that my views were essentially conservative. I didn't want to look outside the Northeast for new opportunities. I believed in my vision from 1991, that we could emerge as the top energy supplier in the Northeast and that that would be a significant accomplishment. I believed that sometimes it is what you don't do rather than what you do that can mean the difference between success and failure. Most of my decisions at that time proved to be the right ones. I made some that weren't so good. I got us into the unregulated gas and electric marketing business in an attempt to compete with the Enrons of the world. But that business has proven to be a disappointment, unable to sustain itself profitably. We discovered, for example, that despite the promises of deregulation, most customers don't like having a choice when it comes to energy and services. They liked getting everything from one source and took comfort in the regulated utilities.

So with all this, I didn't have much time to sit and reflect on what was happening. There was too much to do. But I did wonder every so often whether I was up to the daunting task. It was a difficult undertaking, and I had never done anything like this before. I was aware that some in the business community thought I might be too much of a "nice guy" to have the toughness that was required. I couldn't allow that to hinder me. I prayed for strength, but I also had faith that things would work out. I have always been an optimist and felt that if I really worked at something, applied myself, and engaged the people around me, things would work out. I decided to let business history decide whether I was tough enough.

Of course, what most people tend to forget during the trauma of mergers is that you still have to do business. You still have gas pipes to lay in the ground and downed electrical lines to repair after snowstorms. I can honestly say that I'm never as proud of my employees as I am when they perform under great duress. I always make it a point to thank people for their outstanding work every time I address an employee group. It is not pandering or currying favor; it is deeply heartfelt.

I remember vividly a visit I made to one of our Long Island electric plants during the summer after the merger. David Manning, my new senior vice president of corporate affairs, was accompanying me to a television interview during an intense summer heat wave, a long stretch of days above 90 degrees. In the car, after the interview, David got a call that one of our nearby plants had gone down due to the overwhelming demand for electricity that day. There was a rather spectacular failure of a feedwater pump that shut down one of the units and reduced the plant's capacity to about half at a time when every kilowatt was crucial.

I decided to stop by and see how they handled the crisis. David called the plant to tell them we would be arriving shortly, which was about the last thing they wanted to deal with at that moment. Surprise CEO visits are always dicey, but a visit during a crisis is particularly stressful. But I wasn't going there to conduct an unannounced inspection. I honestly wanted to observe how my people handled difficult situations and let them know that I was aware of how hard they had been working. Most of all, I wanted them to know they had my support.

The plant was hot, noisy, and oppressive, and everyone was racing around trying to fix the problem. I donned a hard hat and spent an hour talking to people, watching them do the repairs, asking a few questions, and letting my engineering background show through. I mostly tried to stay out of the way. After their initial discomfort, the crew saw that I was simply there as a cheerleader, not an interrogator. I actually love going out in the field and seeing how crews handle their jobs. I was once out there myself, at least on the gas side, and you never forget where you came from. At least, you shouldn't. And when I left the electric plant that day, I could feel that I had won over some people. They were genuinely pleased at our encounter and had a chance to see me just as I had seen them. Most important, they did the repair in record time, and the unit was back on line in two days.

As I walked through the heat and humidity back to my car that day, I felt the first rumblings of satisfaction and hope. This merger, like everything else I had ever done in my life, was a journey. The journey moves forward and evolves; the scenery changes and there are inevitable detours. I sensed that it was going to take these kind of encounters, hundreds of them, thousands of them, among me, my officers, and the employees, in order for this marriage to become solid and strong. It would be difficult. We would probably lose some people along the way. But we had crossed a threshold, and suddenly the gnawing seeds of doubt disappeared. For me, the KeySpan I'd envisioned had truly and finally come to life.

The Monk

*G*etting a company to realize the financial and operational benefits of a merger is a difficult job, one not easily accomplished by a CEO alone. Even hiring a monk with divine connections won't do much good. What's behind the success of any corporate venture is employee commitment, their willingness to get personally involved, work together, and make it all happen. It's something that can't be commanded or coerced. Commitment can only be invited.

Finding ways to secure that commitment and to create a corporate environment that connects employee passion to business needs is a major challenge. After the merger, I spent a good percentage of my time working on that. In fact, I still do today.

After the dust settled on the controversy, Bob was concerned about the level of disruption that had overtaken the company in the past few months. "I'm worried that all this turmoil will distract employees from the business," he told me. "You may need to turn your collar around for this effort and get divine support. The merger has generated unrest and confusion. Now's the time to bring employees together. I need you to work on this."

One of the first and most important opportunities to address this issue emerged in the company's information technology (IT) group. KeySpan had promised the state of New York that the merger would produce $1 billion in savings over the first 10 years of the deal. Much of these savings were contingent on the successful implementation of computer technology. Technology would be used to automate large portions of the business, produce synergy savings, and ultimately reduce costs to the customers.

Many of these savings were connected to the work of our technology staff. But getting the 400 IT employees from Brooklyn and Long Island to work together to make cost-effective decisions and adopt unified computer systems throughout the company was a monumental task. The two groups had been at odds with each other since the merger began, each believing that its approach and solutions were superior.

I often thought that Catholics were the only ones with strong beliefs and dogmatic stances. Computer people are even worse. Their adherence to one technology over another is cause for inflicting another series of Crusades upon the world. Those who dare differ with the prevailing beliefs are branded as heretics and condemned to hell.

The chief information officer (CIO) was desperate and called me in to assist. "I want the bickering and fighting to stop," he said. "They need to get beyond their myopic self-interest or we'll never meet our financial commitment." He planned on getting the entire department together for a threat-filled, hour-long meeting, and he offered me a 10-minute slot on the agenda to convince them of the evil of their ways.

"Just because I was a monk doesn't mean that I can perform miracles," I reminded him. Besides, I doubted if there was anything I could say that would change things. I believed that the solution resided not with me but with the employees themselves. I offered the CIO a plan. "When you bring them together, why not give them the opportunity to work the problems out on their own?"

My idea was to host a daylong "Open Space" event for the entire department. Open Space is a popular organizational change model I had read about that brings large groups of people together with no particular agenda beyond the commitment and the energy of the participants. It is based on the monastic belief that one person with passion is worth more than 99 with good ideas. In Open Space, people come together, design and attend sessions of their own choosing, and are individually responsible for running the event and generating practical solutions. It is a creative, chaotic, and extremely energizing experience.

"Let's put the focus where it belongs: on them," I told the CIO.

Keep in mind that as a technologist, he was extremely skeptical of me and my work. That he came to me at all demonstrated how serious his situation was. He was intrigued with the concept but wanted some reassurance.

"You're asking me to invest a lot of time and money for this event," he said. "Have you ever done anything like this before?" The truth of the matter was no. Many of the events I did for the company I had never done before. That hadn't stopped me in the past. I had read about Open Space and understood that it entailed bringing large groups of people together. Many who attend bring a mixture of discouragement and hope for a better future. A select few might even hope for divine inspiration to find a creative solution. The facilitator's role is to serve the needs of the participants and largely stay out of the way, so that those with some passion can get to the work at hand.

In short, Open Space involves hundreds of people sitting in a circle, many of them wounded and looking for hope, and all with an unstated request for godly help. To me, it all sounded a lot like a Catholic Mass. I had held many of those before, with far more than 400 people. Besides, Bob had often encouraged me to try new things to reshape the way we conduct business. "Trust me," I said. "I've done things like this before on many occasions. If the employees want it to work, it will."

We rented out all the ballroom and conference space in the Garden City Hotel on Long Island for the day. After the CIO's brief introduction, I stepped in front of 400 IT employees seated in a circle in the hotel's Grand Ballroom.

"The focus of today's program is on you and how best to meet the company's business needs." I told them that there was no formal agenda beyond this. "I'm not in charge of the day. You are." Outside the ballroom we had reserved 20 conference rooms for any of the self-managed breakout sessions that employees volunteered to host. "There will be no moderator or facilitator," I informed them. "The plan is for you to manage yourselves and identify the tasks that you think need to get accomplished."

Most of the audience looked skeptical, believing it to be another ploy to implement management's agenda. I plunged ahead anyway. "I invite those who would like to to come up to the microphone, state your passion, and sign your name on the list of breakout rooms so you can host your session."

I saw 400 heads swiveling around, looking for some brave soul to step forward. Hundreds of professional people sitting in a circle, enveloped in stillness, is a rare corporate event. Silence, while soothing to me, is unnerving to most business folks. I let that be as it may and hoped it would work in my favor. As the quiet intensified, it propelled one courageous employee forward to the microphone.

"My name is Bill Kearns," he said. "I'd like to host a session discussing the relocation of the company's call center." I instructed him to sign his name on the bulletin board next to a conference room and wait on the side. "Anyone else have a topic that needs to be discussed?" Another employee stepped to the microphone. "I'm Michael Greene, and I want to host a session about using the Internet to better meet our business needs." He walked over and signed his name next to another room.

The floodgates opened. Within 20 minutes, 53 employees volunteered to host sessions. Topics ranged from "Where should we consolidate the data center?" to "How can we allow more employees to work from their homes?" As one programmer said at the end of the day, "I was surprised how the energy in the room shifted once we realized that we were truly in charge of the day."

Every employee who hosted a session was responsible for capturing the main recommendations that came out of the discussion and reporting them back to the group. If a person didn't like a particular session, he or she was free to leave and join another. A few found none of the sessions satisfactory and spent the remainder of the day creating their own. We underestimated the level of employee involvement and ran out of conference rooms in which to meet. Impassioned employees started hosting sessions at the bar, around the piano, and in the hallways. One large group of computer technicians took advantage of the sunny day and moved their meeting of 50 people to an outside gazebo.

"This is the first time I've ever been at a corporate meeting that didn't have an agenda or senior management telling us what to do," said one of the supervisors. "I felt like I was personally responsible for getting our department to work together. I liked that feeling."

The end result of the Open Space event was the generation of over 200 suggestions for engaging employees' talent and passion to help the company reach its billion-dollar savings commitment. Though the event didn't magically resolve all conflict, it did provide the first real bridges to solidifying the organization into a single, unified group. The Open Space event essentially transferred ownership of the business problem from the CIO to his employees.

"I was very surprised how productive all the chaos was," said the CIO. "They seemed to take charge of the entire day. And the business solutions they came up with were practical and real." He was able to prioritize the group's recommendations and implement a business plan that engaged their energy and commitment. He told me later that he had become a believer. I was very flattered and very relieved. But I was only just getting started.

When faith and hope have been wounded in a company, there's no quick fix to remedy the situation. It takes time, prayer, and ongoing effort to turn the tide. While some company events like Open Space can be large-scale and include hundreds of employees, healing a corporate community after a difficult merger often requires more frequent and smaller meetings.

At Bob's request I worked with Craig Matthews in hosting informal meetings with employees. These were biweekly sessions of 20 employees from Brooklyn and Long Island, and we named them "Face to Face." (You will have noticed by now that we love naming things. I feel it gives our ideas more focus and legitimacy.)

We focused the conversation on employees' hopes and fears and sought to identify pockets of support as well as obstacles that were still present in the mending corporation. The sessions were primarily designed to hear what employees had to say. Craig's introduction made the intent clear: "I'm not here to solve. I'm here to listen. We've all just come through a difficult time, and it will take a while for us and the company to mend."

Craig's willingness to gather employees together, invite their feedback, and offer a nonjudgmental ear had a favorable impact in strengthening the corporate community. It also provided him with timely information about where he needed to give attention in smoothing out the merger transition.

For example, the new corporate policy on the use of company cars came under severe criticism from the employees. The costs to individual employees had been increased significantly, and there was widespread dismay. "I know you don't like the policy, but it's very much in line with the best practices of other companies," was Craig's reply. After repeatedly hearing how divisive this policy had become, however, he was moved to reconsider his decision. "I'm changing the policy," Craig announced at the next Face to Face meeting. "I don't often do that. But these meetings showed me how negatively our workers feel about this. The loss of your morale doesn't offset the money we are saving."

Employees began to see that in the new corporate culture, even though they didn't always have a final say on decisions, they did have influence. As one of our field-workers told me: "I was initially skeptical of meeting with the president. I didn't think he'd really listen to what we had to say. But when he actually changed a corporate policy based on our feedback, I became a believer."

At the end of each meeting, employees were asked to anonymously write down the name of an employee who represented what is best about KeySpan. "The employees are our best judges of character," he said. "Let them nominate the candidates." Craig would then send a personal note of thanks to those people at their homes.

A few days after each Face to Face session, letters from the president arrived. "Your name has recently come to my attention as a person who represents what's best about KeySpan," the note started. "It's people like you that make this company a success and I personally thank you for your efforts. Please accept the enclosed $100 gift certificate as a small token of my appreciation." The letter ended with an invitation: "If you'd like to know more about how your name got selected, please call Kenny Moore."

Once these letters began arriving, my phone started to ring. "I got this letter from the president and thought I was being fired," a technical trainer told me. "But he was actually thanking me. I showed it to my wife and kids. They were amazed." Several employees cried when they spoke with me. Said one of our phone representatives, "I always try to do my job in a quiet way. I'm basically a shy person and don't look for recognition. This note touched something deep inside me and let me know that my quiet efforts don't go unnoticed."

One field supervisor framed the letter and hung it in his kitchen. They all wanted to know how their names got chosen. I explained the process—that anonymous co-workers had submitted their names. "I don't know what you did to deserve it, but whatever it was, keep it up," I urged them. "You're making the company a grand place to work!"

Though the troops were having difficulty with the merger, our managers were likewise suffering through a difficult transition. The company, in its postmerger state, had significantly grown and new relationships had to be forged. For me the task ahead was to continue on in building a business community, but now on a grander scale. A further aspect of my challenge was to accomplish that in an engaging and entertaining way.

At another of my "take it for what it's worth" sessions with Bob, I shared with him what I was hearing from the company's directors. "The merger is demoralizing people. Some feel like it's no longer fun to work here. Others say that with all the activity, they have no time left for learning." I explained that I wanted to do something that was business related, but fun, something connected to the work at hand but that would provide our leaders with new business skills.

I was no longer amazed when Bob approved my improv event with Izzy Gesell. He had come to trust my judgment, and I had usually been able to demonstrate the value of my ideas, no matter how far out in left field they were. Improv caught my attention because it was a combination of humor and discipline. KeySpan had more than its fair share of discipline: accountants, supervisors, and engineers. What we lacked was a sense of humor in the face of challenging circumstances.

When Bob himself got up to participate in the improv event, it sent a strong message. Everyone needed to step up and make change happen, everyone including the CEO. When Bob flubbed his improv assignment, there was a tense moment. Would he be embarrassed? What should Izzy do to address the moment?

"Mistakes are part of life," Izzy said, deftly. "As business leaders, you need to do more than just place blame. You need to incorporate them into the project. If you don't, everyone will give up trying." His exercises taught us to be supportive of human error and learn how to incorporate imperfections into a less-than-perfect business world.

Charlie Parker, the jazz musician, once said: "If you don't live it, it won't come out your horn." I felt Bob and his executive team distinguished themselves that day by participating on the stage. Inviting employees to take risks and attempt new behaviors is all fine executive talk, but modeling it—even in an imperfect way—is motivating.

"When they actually got on stage and made mistakes just the same as everyone else," said one operating manager, "I knew these guys were serious. They didn't just talk about it. They were willing to get up there, look silly, and take a chance at it. I left the meeting feeling like I could at least do the same thing back with my staff."

As Bob publicly worked at learning some new skills, he was a source of encouragement to the hundreds who sat before him. "If I can do it, so can you," he said in his closing remarks. Slowly, sometimes painfully, KeySpan was morphing into the entity we hoped it could be. I felt that my efforts were actually making a difference and could only marvel at the strange and wonderful confluence of events that had brought me to this place at this time.

CHAPTER SEVEN

~

The New Millennium

I pass with relief from the tossing sea of Cause and Theory to the firm ground of Result and Fact.

—Winston Churchill

On a balmy June night in 2001, for the first time in 44 years, a professional baseball team from Brooklyn took the field to begin its home season. Though it was a single A minor league team, the Brooklyn Cyclones were the toast of Brooklyn that night, and the 7,500 seats at sparkling new KeySpan Park were filled with cheering, happy fans. Throwing out first balls prior to the game were Fred Wilpon, Brooklyn native and owner of the New York Mets, the major league affiliate of the Cyclones; New York Mayor Rudy Giuliani; and Bob Catell, chairman and CEO of KeySpan.

Bringing professional baseball back to Brooklyn had long been a dream of many influential Brooklynites, including Catell. He vividly remembered people crying in the streets and the pain felt when the beloved Dodgers left for Los Angeles in 1957. He had worked for years with various politicians and community groups to try to lure a major league team back to the borough. But the presence of the Yankees and Mets made that an impossible quest.

When Giuliani, himself an unapologetic baseball fanatic, took office in the early 1990s, the possibility of bringing minor league baseball into the city suddenly became real. Giuliani worked with Yankees owner George Steinbrenner to unveil a minor league Yankees affiliate on Staten Island. After that, he persuaded Wilpon to do the same with the Mets in Brooklyn.

The decision to put a new ballpark on Surf Avenue in Coney Island met with tremendous enthusiasm. And when KeySpan was approached about supplying its name to the new park, Catell didn't hesitate. For him, this was a natural connection. KeySpan had a strong relationship with the Mets and Shea Stadium. Not only would this move help bring baseball back to Brooklyn, but it would provide substantial public relations opportunities for KeySpan to spread its image and build its brand.

Catell determined that KeySpan had to secure the naming rights. Not only would the new park bring meaningful economic development to a blighted area of Brooklyn, but it would associate KeySpan with something very positive: the return of baseball. More than anything, it reflected Catell's belief in giving back to the community. He felt deeply, from his earliest experiences at Brooklyn Union, that a company had an obligation to give back something to the community it serves. More than just a publicly held business, KeySpan, for Catell, was a public trust.

After extensive negotiations, KeySpan inked a 20-year deal with the team. The positive public relations far surpassed anything Catell envisioned. The team has sold out every home game since its inception. With the Atlantic Ocean just beyond the right field wall and the bright lights of Coney Island's amusement park over the left field wall, KeySpan Park has become an urban field of dreams, further burnishing the company's positive image as it made the transition from Brooklyn Union. Opening night held its magic to the very end. Trailing the Mahoning Valley Scrappers 2–0 in the bottom of the ninth, the Cyclones' third baseman Edgar Rodriguez lined a two-run, game-tying home run. The Cyclones won it on a sacrifice fly in the bottom of the tenth inning, which sent the fans home happy.

Catell was standing near the railing during the game when a little girl approached with a piece of paper and asked for his autograph. He laughed and asked her why she would want his autograph. "I'm not famous," he told her. Sheepishly, the girl retreated to where her father was standing. Catell walked over, and the man said, "You're Bob Catell, the chairman of KeySpan, aren't you?" Catell nodded. "Well, don't you own this park?" "No, we don't own it," Catell replied, smiling. "But if your daughter wants my autograph, I'm happy to give it to her."

That he was considered a celebrity in his home borough of Brooklyn should not have surprised Catell. In the three years since the LILCO merger, he had emerged as one of the most influential business leaders in New York, having won widespread respect for the way he handled the LILCO situation and for spurring the new company into unprecedented growth. KeySpan was now a Fortune 500 company and a significant player in the energy industry.

At 64, an age when most executives are contemplating retirement, Catell had been energized by his tenure as the leader of a $6 billion organization. To a large degree, he'd fulfilled the goal he had articulated a decade earlier when he first became chief executive of Brooklyn Union: to become the premier energy company in the Northeast. He had taken a major step in that direction in November, when he engineered a $2.5 billion acquisition of Eastern Enterprises, the largest gas supplier in Massachusetts.

That acquisition, though geographically more challenging, had been less complex than the LILCO merger. Absent were the contentious leadership issues and culture shifts that occurred with LILCO. Eastern Enterprises, an amalgam of smaller, independent gas companies that had been themselves acquired by the former Boston Gas, was far more amenable to the takeover. Catell had long-standing relationships with the key executives at Eastern. The Boston Gas culture had broad similarities to that of Brooklyn Union—long history, employee-centric, community-oriented—so the integration had been, to some degree, faster and smoother than with LILCO.

But coming so quickly on the heels of the LILCO earthquake, the Eastern acquisition felt to KeySpan like a strong aftershock. Here were yet another 2,000 new KeySpan employees, from a distant and unfamiliar territory, who had to be assimilated into the organization. Coupled with nearly 3,000 new employees who joined as part of newly acquired unregulated businesses, the company's population had soared. What it said to everyone in dramatic and conclusive fashion was: The company we once knew is truly gone.

The new acquisition created further chaos and uncertainty for the weary and stressed troops, still trying to absorb the creation of KeySpan. It is difficult to underestimate the tectonic shifts that occur in an organization that undergoes such dramatic growth and change in such a short period. Where once the company was small enough to be self-contained and where everyone knew everyone else's name, now there was a very different playing field.

One of the major traumas was that there were suddenly many people in different jobs. Existing jobs changed to fit the new environment, and at the same time people took new positions outside their old disciplines. At meetings, new people showed up with skill sets that might or might not be comparable to the skills of those who had held such positions in the past. Many began to ask, "How do I fit in?"

For those in human resources, like Elaine Weinstein, there was a steady procession of people who were having difficulty adjusting. People were sometimes shaky in their new roles or felt they were not getting the respect that should be afforded them. With mergers, positions are often divided or reframed so that someone might lose a piece of their former responsibilities, and that would open the door to new levels of office politics, backstabbing, and undermining that had been generally absent from Brooklyn Union.

"This was really a human laboratory," Weinstein says. "You got to see how relationships shifted, what new organisms emerged. As people got to know each other, they started to realize that a person might have talent they never knew about. Some were accepting, some were not."

For Kenny Moore, the march of progress and growth presented endless counterpoints to his search for meaning in the corporate world. In 1999, with the LILCO integration finally moving forward,

Catell named Moore corporate ombudsman. The ombudsman role had long been commonplace in such institutions as the military, hospitals, and governmental agencies. But now it had begun to seep into corporations, where it would find varying degrees of acceptance.

In a memo to all employees, Catell wrote: "Kenny is uniquely qualified for this work," specifying Moore's dedication to the "corporate common good." He made it clear that Moore's role was neutral, confidential, and, most of all, influential with him. "I am optimistic about this initiative and invite you to talk openly and honestly with Kenny. I will be meeting regularly with him to further understand patterns and organizational trends that will require action or redress. This information is of paramount importance for us in order to change and grow."

Now that what had already been in place for several years was formalized, Moore's credibility soared, as did his popularity. He found his office becoming more and more of a destination for both staffers and officers seeking his insight and calm reflection. His corner office, high above the streets of Brooklyn, was purposely distant from the executive floor. People noticed immediately that his office had a different look and feel, just a bit more warm and inviting than the traditional corporate office. Bob Fani, a once-skeptical officer, noticed the artwork and poems on the walls and the way the space was set up to be relaxing, not threatening. "It creates an atmosphere where you want to communicate and you want to share," Fani says. "There are times when I need to speak to Kenny and I'll go his office rather than have him come to mine, which is more traditional and structured. I just feel we can speak more openly there."

With troops now scattered across the Northeast, many could not visit Moore's office personally. But as word spread about his role and his effectiveness, his voice mail and e-mail boxes were generally filled on a daily basis with plaintive calls from people struggling to embrace the uncertainty that always accompanies change.

The metamorphosis of KeySpan into a major corporate entity took a toll on people in overt and subtle ways. Moore had observed in recent years that people's jobs had taken on new levels of meaning and importance, more so than they had in the past. The social structures that had anchored people's lives—marriage, church and synagogue, community involvement, neighborhoods—had become less influential or even disappeared for many people over the past decade or more. Divorce rates had increased, religious worship declined, volunteerism and community involvement, even in an enlightened company like KeySpan, had leveled off, becoming less relevant than the lure of the New Economy. Yet just as work became the focus of attention, companies began to reengineer, downsize, and embrace technology that emphasized smaller, more empowered workforces. Suddenly, the work-as-family concept came under increasing fire as corporate loyalty became an anachronistic catchphrase from a bygone era.

No wonder people felt lost, marginalized, uncertain about so many things that had once seemed so solid and grounded. Moore understood these feelings viscerally from his work in the church. He had a way of listening to people's pain and offering comfort without resorting to clichés.

The gatherings he orchestrated around the company, from Employee Care meetings to Break Bread dinners, were all aimed at creating forums for people to open up and express their feelings. Healing can only begin, he felt, when a person can acknowledge these feelings in a supportive, caring environment.

In one such meeting on Long Island, Moore encountered a group of former LILCO union workers who were grappling with the aftereffects of deregulation. One of the casualties of deregulation was KeySpan's appliance repair business. No longer able to both sell the gas and electricity as well as offer repair services, the company had to spin off the service businesses into unregulated entities. For many longtime employees, this meant choosing between staying with the regulated utility or leaving for an unfamiliar new company.

One veteran technician had chosen to stay with the utility but, to his dismay, his supervisor had come to collect his repair tools. No one had ever taken away his tools before and he was shaken by the experience. The tools had become an extension of him. Having someone take them away felt like a personal violation, almost like an amputation. When he spoke to Moore and the group, his poignant sadness resonated with others who shared their own fears and concerns with him. To find a corporate setting where one can talk about such deep feelings in a public forum without fear of ridicule or judgment is the key, according to Moore. Being able to release the burden is the first step toward healing and moving forward.

"Part of the work I do is to create a safe space for people to be who they are, where they are, experience what they are experiencing—and it's okay," Moore explains. "Then they are more able to feel free to move on."

In his tenure as ombudsman, Moore has noticed an increase in activity during periods of transition. After the Eastern merger, Catell sent him out to broker new relationships in New England and build trust in places where trust would become a crucial commodity over time. Moore understood that such activity must be ongoing and consistent; it can't be a one-time meeting or conversation. Having Catell announce to the entire company that Moore reported directly to him created a legitimacy that provided a foundation for all of his work. People understood that he was not a lone maverick wandering the halls of KeySpan on some secret mission.

Moore's status rose among the most skeptical ranks as well, the corporate executives. Those who had rolled their eyes when first meeting Moore had long since been won over. Bob Fani remembers the early cynicism, not unexpected in an engineering organization, with regard to this freethinker who openly expressed emotion and caring. Early experiences like the corporate funeral got people thinking about the unusual view of the world that Moore espoused.

Over the years, Fani has not only embraced Moore's role but has actively promoted Moore's importance to colleagues both inside KeySpan and in other companies. He tells them about Moore's unique contribution and effectiveness and even shows people the odd and offbeat "job description" that Moore created at Fani's behest when they were discussing Moore's career development path. Unlike a traditional resume or job posting, Moore's eclectic document talked broadly about connecting to people rather than pigeonholing himself into boxes and charts and chains of command. "His job description told me that he was different and his contribution has to be different," Fani says. He has made copies of the job description to give to colleagues and challenges them: "Does your HR organization have this perspective?"

Fani is often asked to comment on the benefits of having someone like Moore in the organization. He explains that in today's corporate environment, there will inevitably be times when employees simply won't want to talk to someone in the chain of command, even HR, about issues and problems that swirl around them. To them, the people who typically solve such problems may no longer be the right people, due to either insensitivity, politics, or an increasing sense of alienation and lack of feelings of loyalty.

Even though the HR function provides a legitimacy, an organizational tie-in to Moore's work, Moore doesn't represent the traditional organization. His neutrality allows him to maintain strict confidentiality concerning matters that are brought to his attention without necessarily having to act on them, as HR might be required to do. Such autonomy, coupled with Moore's appealing style and charisma, draws a steady flow of pilgrims seeking corporate salvation.

For Catell, years of working with the ex-monk created a strange yet comfortable synergy. His intense desire to move the company forward often butted up against the next outlandish idea that Kenny conceived. When Moore told him, for example, that he intended to include several moments of quiet meditation in an upcoming meeting, Catell blanched. As an engineer, such touchy-feely fare was antithetical. It was, in fact, the last thing an engineer would think of to repair a problem. An engineer would attempt to fix a predicament through formulas and mathematical equations.

Nonetheless, as Moore became established as an effective facilitator, Catell went along with the exercise. Realizing it would create doubt and incredulity in some minds—"the old man has really lost it this time"—he gave the nod to Moore and ignored the rolling eyes and smirks of the few cynics in the room. "We needed something," Catell recalled. "There wasn't a lot of downside risk, and it was worth a try."

Then, in January 2001, as KeySpan was grappling with all its growing pains, Kenny Moore stepped off the treadmill in his New Jersey home and felt an odd sensation across his chest and down his arms. He grew lightheaded and sat on the edge of his bed. He told his wife Cynthia that he was supposed to be heading to Boston in an hour for meetings but maybe she ought to call an ambulance instead.

His heart attack was significant. He refused to blame it on the stress of the job, instead citing family history and his own life-threatening bout with cancer many years earlier. Regardless of its origin, Moore ended up with a quadruple bypass and yet another encounter with his own mortality. He would spend the next three months recuperating at home. The company mobilized its support for Moore, offering everything he would need to get through his ordeal. In a culture that is warm, embracing, and as longevity-based as KeySpan's, support for employees in personal crisis is a vital part of corporate values. A generous benefits package coupled with the genuine concern and support of management was a Brooklyn Union trait that continues at KeySpan. The culture says that not only is it the right thing to do but it creates intensely loyal employees.

Being known and generally beloved by the KeySpan population, Moore engendered great compassion and a widespread outpouring of concern and affection. "It was a loss when he wasn't here," Weinstein says. From the officers to the union workers, people reached out to offer help and support.

Catell was hit hard by Moore's illness, not only because of his personal relationship but because he knew there would be a tremendous vacuum created by his absence. He believed that Moore's work had created such widespread value that he would be there in spirit throughout his recuperation.

The year 2001 was shaping up to be a difficult year anyway. The economy showed no signs of recovering anytime soon. An especially warm winter in the Northeast had wreaked havoc with the company's revenues. And in New England, where local regulations disallowed the kind of weather normalization guidelines that utilities could invoke in New York, the incentive bonuses were painfully small. Just a year into the acquisition, the New England contingent felt angry and cheated as their colleagues to the south received fatter bonus checks. Winning their souls became that much harder.

As the summer reached toward Labor Day, Catell had a small bright spot to enjoy in an otherwise bleak landscape. The Brooklyn Cyclones, in their first year of existence, were enjoying a stellar season. On September 12, they were slated to play for the league championship. But events of the day before not only caused the cancellation of the game, but changed the world forever.

The CEO

~

I think it's fair to say that the new millennium didn't start off as the corporate world had anticipated it would. The dreams and optimism associated with this historic moment quickly soured. Just months into 2000, the bottom began to fall out of what had been the hottest economic expansion in history. By the middle of 2001, the Internet bubble hadn't so much burst as exploded, the economy continued to slide, and the fallout spread across every sector and every industry.

The energy industry entered a particularly bleak period during the summer of 2000 as the California energy crisis demonstrated that deregulation, which had many of its origins in California, not only did not work as anticipated but actually led to rolling blackouts and fiscal chaos. I sensed that trouble was on the horizon for some of the energy giants.

When the Enron scandal broke the following year, only months after Enron CEO Jeff Skilling had warned us that we would soon become dinosaurs if we stuck to our current business models, there was no small sense of irony. I certainly felt a twinge of vindication, but I knew that the outbreak of corporate malfeasance and executive corruption was going to blanket our entire industry with a black cloud. No matter how great a reputation we had, we were going to be lumped together with the bad guys.

Having survived the LILCO crisis and having initiated the Eastern Enterprises acquisition, I had great confidence in what we were building within KeySpan. Yet I cannot remember a more difficult time to be a CEO, because everything I personally believed in as a human being as well as an executive seemed to be flowing into contradictions. As CEO of a public company, my first responsibility is to the shareholders. Keeping the Wall Street financial community satisfied is an endless and often thankless proposition. Every quarter is a new test. Keeping costs in line sometimes requires unpleasant measures, such as workforce reductions. But if you disappoint the Street, you get severely punished and your shareholders suffer. When your shares get hammered because of the mistakes of other companies, however, there is nothing but frustration and aggravation. All a CEO can do is put aside the emotion and continue to execute the strategic vision.

I honestly believe that it is during the toughest times that you have to fall back on your basic values rather than abandon them. That is why I elevated Kenny to a formal position as corporate ombudsman. I wanted to make clear to everyone that the soul of this company was honored and nurtured, and that I wasn't just paying lip service to a program du jour but honestly believed that the value Kenny brought to me and to the company had a very real impact on the bottom line.

For all of my tenure as chairman, I'd always been able to count on my conviction that a dedicated and loyal workforce performs far better than an angry and disillusioned one. All my efforts with Kenny to find the spiritual center of our company were based on this premise. When your workers perform to the best of their capabilities, the company does well and the shareholders benefit. So while it has always been about compassion and doing the right thing, that philosophy hasn't been in place just to make me feel good about myself. I do it because it is in the best interests of the people who truly own this company. And given that most of our employees are shareholders as well, the benefits come full circle.

But here in the new millennium, things simply got harder to accomplish; the tests became more challenging, and the choices more problematic. With KeySpan, now a massive new entity trying to coalesce into a growing and profitable enterprise, the challenges became greater and more difficult. Sending Kenny and other top officers out into the field, up to New England as emissaries carrying a simple message was one of the first things I did as we completed the Eastern deal.

The Eastern Enterprises acquisition had taken up the bulk of my time in 2000. Coming on the heels of LILCO, it set off waves of anxiety and uncertainty for a group still trying to adjust to the first merger. I weighed that concern against the tremendous benefit I envisioned over the long term, which was the basis for the deal. Opportunities to grow into a big enough and powerful enough entity to remain independent had to be taken seriously. I believed we could derive greater value for our shareholders through growth than by becoming a takeover candidate.

We had a deep understanding of this marketplace. We owned significant assets here and it was the ideal marketplace for an energy company: huge population, affluent customer base, cold weather to support the gas business, and a relatively low penetration of gas customers, all of which provided opportunity for growth. I watched some of our competitors opt to target other areas of the United States and even make investments in international operations. Enron, for example, invested billions in a power plant in India, a move that eventually proved unsustainable. For me, our greatest opportunity was closer to home.

Over the course of a decade, I had established a solid relationship with Woody Ives, the chairman of Eastern Enterprises and its major subsidiary, Boston Gas. I told him when I first met him that if he ever thought about a merger, Brooklyn Union and Boston Gas would make a great combination. When he called me in August 2000 to tell me that he was ready to sell, it was an opportunity I couldn't pass up. I was hoping over the years to make a quiet deal with him for a lower price, but he told me he had to put Eastern up for bid. And this is where relationships mean so much. We didn't make the highest bid, but after many conversations with Woody it became clear that our culture and the way we treated people played a major role in his decision. I also knew he respected me and the way I did business and that this merger would create value for his shareholders. Some financial people think we overpaid anyway, but to me, this was a no-brainer. I would have been extremely disappointed to see someone else gain control of Eastern.

We added 800,000 gas customers to our rolls, which brought us up to 2.5 million gas customers, the most in the Northeast. Yet the 800,000 represented just 40 percent of the potential marketplace, which meant we had tremendous upside potential in New England.

We also elevated the stress levels at KeySpan. Incorporating yet another new entity meant another head count reduction. We eliminated 300 jobs through attrition and early retirement programs. The problem you encounter with early retirement programs is that you end up losing some of the good people you would prefer to retain. It was apparent to me that we couldn't count on early retirement programs as a fallback for every workforce reduction in the future. At the same time, I was unwilling to resort to wholesale layoffs. I had made promises to our people and to our unions, and I was determined to avoid layoffs. My hope was to grow the business enough to avoid the need for layoffs now and in the future.

At the same time, we also had to introduce ourselves to Massachusetts. I spent a lot of time meeting with regulators and elected officials in order to establish KeySpan as a credible entity. I've always enjoyed the political relationship building associated with a government-regulated business. Dating back to my days as vice president of the rate and regulatory side of Brooklyn Union in the 1970s, I learned quickly that much of what is accomplished in this sector occurs in the halls and anterooms of the State House.

Back then, Woody Dunlop, my fellow Brooklyn Union executive, was my mentor. He was extremely knowledgeable and savvy, and he taught me how to work the political process. I learned valuable lessons from him about what to say and how to say it, and about keeping my cool in difficult situations. Early on, I would get upset when I had made a very logical and sound case to the regulators in Washington or Albany, only to be rejected. Woody taught me that logic doesn't always prevail and that you have to look for compromises. You have to look at the situation from the regulators' standpoint and find that subtle place where you satisfy them while getting what you need.

After several years in that arena, I understood what Woody meant. It is an art form, an acquired skill, and I found that I was good at it. It has served me and the company well over the years. I honestly felt that the regulators were colleagues and should be treated as such. And while I was on a first-name basis with most of the regulators and politicians in Albany, I had to start fresh in Massachusetts. I felt I had an advantage here because of KeySpan's impeccable track record in New York. The most valuable lesson I had learned over the years was that regardless of how good you might be at building relationships, there was no substitute for a solid reputation as an honest, forthright organization. Regulators are human. Given an opportunity to consider all facets of an issue, they will take into account a company's track record in terms of compliance, willingness to acknowledge errors, and the attitudes and behavior of its executives.

Some people think I'm too nice. I've always found great success treating other people the way I want to be treated. I actually don't mind being underestimated occasionally. More often than not, it works in my favor. I believe, for example, that my respect and belief and caring for people come back in the form of intense loyalty and receptivity to my message. Inevitably, that is beneficial to the company. One of our board members, Ed Miller, always tells me that Marines learn that "If you want loyalty up, you've got to give loyalty down." I believe that. And loyalty doesn't mean a willingness to accept mediocrity. I may not enjoy making a tough decision that might mean letting a 25-year veteran go because he is no longer meeting the demands of his position. But I will do it if the situation calls for it. I may not move as quickly as some would like, but after 45 years with the company, I feel pretty comfortable in my own skin. After the LILCO situation, I thought about that old Leo Durocher quote and laughed. Maybe nice guys don't always finish last.

In the business world, however, you can never take your eye off the brand. I got a taste of both the value and fragile nature of a corporate reputation. In February 2000, we had acquired a number of mechanical contracting and engineering services companies in order to build our unregulated energy services business. Perhaps owing to our lack of experience in these markets, we made one acquisition that came back to haunt us.

We had purchased a small contracting firm called Roy Kay, Inc.

that was based in Freehold, New Jersey. We soon realized that the management of that company did not conduct its business in the way that KeySpan felt was appropriate. Eventually, we had to shut the company down and take some significant write-downs for the year. There were some nasty lawsuits filed by the Roy Kay people and shareholders. The publicity surrounding the incident was strident, to say the least.

Not only was it distressing and disappointing but it offered a very blunt and graphic example of how fragile a good name can be. We had spent 100 years building our reputation, and an incident like this cast a shadow over the entire company. The press sometimes reports things in a way that can paint an inaccurate and damaging picture of what happened, yet it becomes difficult to defend yourself without sounding self-serving.

We have always been a very conservative company. We toe the line closely in terms of complying with obligations and following regulations. So when accusations started to fly about our business ethics, it was deeply unsettling. We have a code of ethics that each new employee signs. But you really want people to believe it, not just sign it. You want them to really believe there is a right way to do things and get comfortable with knowing that if there is an issue or they make a mistake they should come forward.

I believe you have to create a culture where you don't shoot the messenger. You want people to feel empowered, to know that they can take risks and that if they fail, they won't get slammed for it. We got past the Roy Kay situation relatively unscathed, but it was a wake-up call for how careful you have to be when you go into a growth mode. Acquisitions can be risky no matter how closely you examine the deal, and sometimes you simply can't know people until you try to work with them.

The Roy Kay incident did have one positive effect: It made me focus even harder on the Eastern integration. We needed to make sure that we correctly handled not only the business side of the deal, but the community-building efforts as well. For example, we set about immediately to start building KeySpan's presence in the community in New England by adding $10 million to the KeySpan Foundation's endowment so that we could contribute to important organizations around the Boston area. We quickly contributed to an after-school program designed to provide places for children to go after school in urban areas.

We also addressed the incentive compensation program for our New England employees. Realizing how upsetting it was for these new KeySpan employees to feel deeply resentful of the low bonus payouts during their first year with the company, we knew we had to make some dramatic changes. Our senior executives met and agreed that because New England could not enjoy the weather normalization benefits that those in New York enjoyed, we would modify our incentive compensation plan in New York to take on some of the risk and pass the benefits on to New England. This was a measure of our culture. We are trying to create a team, a feeling that we are all in this together and that we want our brethren in New England to be part of the KeySpan family, so we are willing to take on some additional risk to make that happen. By 2002, after an excellent performance, New Englanders received significantly higher bonuses, which, at the end of the day, always makes people feel better.

Needless to say, I felt like I had been through the mill during this long, stressful period. And when Kenny suffered his heart attack, not only was I concerned for his health, for his family, and for his role in the organization, but I realized how much I had come to depend on his eyes and ears and heart to provide me invaluable insight into my own company. I couldn't imagine losing that, and I prayed for him to recover.

Being one of those eternal optimists, I essentially refuse to give in to despair. Maybe it means putting some blinders on for a while or maybe it is just my genetic makeup, like some people have blue eyes and blond hair. As 2001 unfolded, with Kenny at home recuperating and the economy refusing to cooperate, I thought I had dug deep into my own reserves for the strength to ride out a difficult period. I honestly believed things would take a turn for the better. And as September approached and Kenny returned to work, there seemed to be some cause for optimism.

Of course, when I left my house on the morning of September 11, a nearly flawless morning out on Long Island, to head to an early meeting in Hicksville, I had no idea that I was beginning what would be the longest day of my life, as it was for so many others, especially in New York City.

The Monk

~

"Part of your value to KeySpan," Bob often reminds me, "is that you have a very different way of approaching work. While some think of it as odd, I find it refreshingly different." He continually invites me to give creativity free rein in the service of supporting employees as well as the business.

Occasionally, I'm inspired by unexpected events to find new ways to provide such service. For my fiftieth birthday, for example, Cyndi presented me with a poster entitled "Life's Little Secrets" that hangs on my office wall. It was her playful attempt to offset a midlife crisis. The poster offers advice like: "Wave at kids on school buses," "Watch one sunrise each year," and "Never refuse homemade brownies." My favorite is: "Send lots of Valentine's Day cards. Sign them 'From someone who thinks you're grand.'"

With Bob's encouragement lingering in my mind, I pondered what would happen if I actually sent cards to employees on this special day. Might it be a small step in nourishing and renewing the heart of our workers? I chose to do more than reflect.

A week before Valentine's Day, I grabbed a box of my son's "Barney" valentines. Even knowing how most adults feel about the purple dinosaur, I took the cards to work and began addressing them. "Thanks for bringing warmth to KeySpan" I wrote in one, "You make a heartfelt difference at work" in another. I got on a roll and finished the whole box of 50 cards.

When Valentine's Day arrived, I was prepared. Coming in early, I walked around the building dropping cards in offices and cubicles, on chairs and workstations. Bob and a handful of executives each got one. A whole bunch went to supervisors and managers. I kept the largest stash for our union workers, the ones who do the majority of the physical work. I figured that 90 percent of the employees who received the cards would think I was crazy. But I believed there would be 10 percent who understood what I was trying to do and might gain some strength of heart from the cards.

The reaction was just the opposite. Large numbers of people responded positively. Craig Matthews, the company's president, replied: "How refreshing. Thank you for noticing."

I got another note from an officer who seldom sees value in much of the work I do: "While I can't go into the details, your card was the high point to an otherwise miserable day. Thanks." I wondered what executive events were going on for him. The management and union folks responded just as warmly. One woman wrote, "This is the first Valentine card I have ever received from a man I've never slept with." I chose to interpret this as a show of gratitude.

Within a day or two, the notes stopped. Life went back to normal; or so I thought. But two months later when I was called into an executive's office to work on a corporate project, there, taped on her wall, was the "Barney" valentine. Upon closer examination, I came to see that a lot of the cards were still pinned on cubicle walls, workstations, and corporate office walls. Sometimes, small gestures have a positive way of lingering.

The following year on Valentine's Day, I sent out a new bunch of cards, and again the year after that. I even received a card myself the last time around: a child's "Alien" valentine with a lollipop attached. My co-worker signed it: "I think you're out of this world." It made my heart smile. I still have it on my desk and won't throw it away. It makes me feel warm and cherished, even a little younger than my true chronological age.

Shortly after the LILCO merger, Bob called me into his office. He asked me to take on the new role of corporate ombudsman for all our management employees. "Employees trust you, and I need you to use that trust in continuing to help them as well as the business," he said. "You've been doing this work unofficially. It's now time to publicly recognize your unique value."

In some ways, this position has parallels to my previous life. It's a job that focuses on the common good and provides our nonunion employees a confidential venue to discuss business problems and personal concerns. The "confessional" nature of the ombudsman role guarantees that what employees discuss remains safeguarded and goes no further than my ears. On an individual level, I offer counsel for dealing with a myriad of problems. On a corporate level, I identify trends and practices that are frustrating the ranks of management and preventing them from fully contributing their talents to the success of the business.

Topics run the gamut from departmental inequities to family tragedies. As one supervisor said to me, "When my husband was diagnosed with cancer, I didn't know where to turn. But since you personally survived cancer and also know HR policies, I thought I'd talk to you first. Besides, I didn't want my co-workers knowing about his illness. I felt guaranteed that our conversation would stay confidential."

In this role, I'm also called in to work on sensitive corporate projects. Steve Zelkowitz, a company executive, was working with a group of African-American employees who had formed an affinity group they called Black Leadership at KeySpan (BLAK).

"I'd like your help in hosting a session between senior management and BLAK," Steve requested. He wanted to make sure that the needs of the company as well as the employees received equal review. He told me that the group had had a couple of meetings and everything was very respectful, but nobody would open up and really share their true thoughts and feelings. Too much was getting bottled up that needed to be out on the table.

I designed a full-day program for the entire council to explore divergent interests. I opened the day by asking the participants to draw a family shield, and on it to list things they liked to do the most and things they disliked to do the most. It was simply a mechanism to get people to open up and start talking. They managed to get many difficult issues out on the table, which led them to form teams and begin the process of addressing those issues. Steve has told me that the event was extremely effective in moving things forward.

As the millennium came to a close, most of KeySpan's activity focused on Y2K concerns and making sure that a business world run by computers wouldn't come crashing to a halt. My interest resided elsewhere. I continued to look for new and engaging ways of building a corporate community as well as keeping Bob in direct contact with the growing number of employees that were populating the company's ranks.

The monthly Break Bread dinner meetings where Bob meets with a handful of our managers not only have a business meaning, they encompass a sacred one as well. Creating and sustaining a company is also partly about creating and sustaining a sense of community. My idea for these meals emanated from the Last Supper: Jesus gathering his disciples together to celebrate community and offer support for the challenges ahead. Though I was certainly not equating Bob with Jesus, I saw useful parallels to the format. Jesus' role had its business counterpart: the CEO gathering employees together over a meal to strengthen the company by fostering community and offering his personal presence. These dinners were a boon to both the business spirit as well as the human one. They were a further manifestation of bringing our vision of the company to fruition. I also came to see that our employees responded favorably.

"I wasn't sure how he was going to react when I criticized the new financial system that we were putting in," said Arthur Abbate, our credit director. "But he was truly appreciative to hear what I had to say. It wasn't just tokenism."

The dinners are intentionally low-key, and most invitees show up not knowing much about the event. "When I got the invitation, I thought I was going to be one of a hundred people," said Lee Reed, who works in the electrical side of the business. "We would never have had something like this back in LILCO." Employees were impressed that Bob would actually stay and host the entire event with such a small group of employees. "When I told my friends that I had an informal dinner with the chairman last week," boasted Jane Judge, "it reminded me how unique this company really is."

At the end of each dinner meeting, Bob asks the participants to write down the name of an employee they feel is an "unsung hero" within the company. He makes it a point to personally call these people to compliment their efforts. "I didn't know what Bob was going to do with the names of the unsung heroes," said one call center director. "Then a few weeks later, my nominee was telling all her co-workers that she'd gotten a phone call from the CEO complimenting her efforts. For the next month, she never stopped taking about it."

I was feeling pretty good about my work and my life as the new millennium unfolded. We often take life for granted when things are going well and we're engaged in meaningful work. Always looming in the background, though, is the specter of death. Woody Allen once said that he didn't mind dying, he just didn't want to be there when it happened. Neither did I, but nonetheless I had my second brush with mortality in the winter of 2001.

As the corporate ombudsman I was continually looking for ways to meet with the employees in New England to introduce myself and support them with the acquisition. On the morning of January 16, as I was about to leave for a morning flight to Boston, I suffered a heart attack. Since my father had collapsed and died in front of me of a massive stroke when I was a boy, I thought heart attacks involved falling unconscious into a convulsive state. Mine was subtler, with dizziness and mild chest pains being the only telltale signs.

The Zen masters preach that what is always speaking silently is the body. Through some divine goodwill, I chose to stop for a moment that morning and listen to what my body was saying. Cyndi called an ambulance, and we wound up in the emergency room of the local hospital.

"Mr. Moore, you're having a heart attack," the doctor informed me after a quick examination. "We're taking you upstairs to put a stent in your artery to unclog it." As they began to wheel me away toward my unknown future, I made one soft request: "Can I kiss my wife before I go?" Even in the midst of medical emergencies, protocol has its flexibility. "We always have time for kisses," the doctor said. A few weeks later, I would be back in the hospital for a quadruple bypass operation, and I was out of work for several months.

Confronting mortality is never an easy task. My bout with cancer in 1986 was my first foray into this deeply human drama. Open-heart surgery was my second. It is both terrifying for the mind, yet therapeutic for the soul. Often in tragedy there is a hidden gift. My surgery gave me another opportunity to closely examine my purpose and place in the world.

I found it both discouraging and heartening to realize that life at KeySpan continued on without me. Charles de Gaulle may have had it right when he said that cemeteries were full of indispensable men. I was humbly reminded that work goes on just fine without me. To believe that I am critical to the running of a business is a mistake. As my spiritual director, Father Theodore, had often reminded me, all of us are valuable but none of us are essential. Bob's support and the kind affection of many employees worked medicinal magic for both my body and soul. As the months passed, I slowly healed and returned to work.

It was while I was recuperating at home that I met Mr. Hatch. He is the main character in the children's book *Somebody Loves You, Mr. Hatch* by Eileen Spinelli (Bradbury Press, 1991), a book that I found myself reading to my sons during my convalescence. It is the story of an isolated working man, who lives, works, and sleeps alone. Neighbors say: "Mr. Hatch likes to keep to himself."

One Saturday he is cleaning his porch when the postman delivers a heart-shaped box of candy with an anonymous note signed "Somebody loves you." Mr. Hatch is confused because he interacts with no one. He finally concludes, "Why, I've got a secret admirer." Mr. Hatch decides to spruce up and walk around town, greeting and helping strangers—all with the hope of meeting the person who sent him the candy. Children are drawn to him. He bakes brownies, serves lemonade, and plays an old harmonica that he has had since his boyhood. Everyone dances. Time passes. Mr. Hatch is having so much fun, he has even forgotten about finding his secret admirer.

Then the postman returns, informs Mr. Hatch that he delivered the candy to the wrong address, and takes back the now-empty box. The "Somebody loves you" note falls out in the transfer, reminding

Mr. Hatch that he was correct at the outset: Nobody really does love him. He withdraws back into his isolation. But the neighborhood kids won't have it. The neighborhood revolts: "We can't let this happen to Mr. Hatch!" Their response is truly extravagant.

The story left me thinking: What would happen if Mr. Hatch showed up at KeySpan? What havoc might be wrought by small gifts, anonymously given to an ordinary worker—possibly even the wrong person? How might my corporate neighbors respond? I decided to find out.

My plan was to anonymously send a $40 floral arrangement to two unsuspecting employees every Monday morning—a Mr. Hatch award. The recipients would be subjectively chosen, sometimes based on their commitment to the corporate common good—or because they just happened to be in the right place at the right time. Attached to the flowers would be a note: "Don't ever think your good efforts go unnoticed." Signed: "From someone who cares."

The business world has taught me to always do a "pilot" before jumping into full implementation. I also learned that it is better to ask for forgiveness than for permission—so I kept the idea to myself and got no formal approval. For my trial run, I picked one employee from the opposite side of my floor, as well as an executive with whom I was working on a special project.

On Monday morning, I walked down to the florist who handles our corporate account and asked what I could get for $40. She showed me a small bowl with five petite flowers in it. (Their overhead must be high.) I told her I wanted to send two arrangements, and to ensure anonymity I would pay cash and I would not sign my name or leave my phone number. The florist was extremely uncomfortable with this. I wasn't feeling too happy about the transaction, either. Maybe this is how all initiators of pilot projects feel?

By that afternoon, the flowers had arrived. I didn't say anything to anyone. On Tuesday I made it a point to pass by the desk of the woman who worked on my floor. I said, "Hey, nice flowers. Is it your birthday?"

"No," she said. "Somebody sent them to me. Look. Here's the note." By this time, all her co-workers were crowded around, telling me the sequence of events. They also knew that an executive got the same flowers delivered. One of them even called the florist to find out who sent it. Nobody seemed to know. They all continued to speak in utter giddiness about the strangeness of the delivery and what made this woman so special. They also spent considerable time trying to figure out what she had in common with the executive, and who might have sent them the flowers.

A few days later, I had a project-update meeting with the executive. I planned to tell him about my pilot as well as get his reaction as a recipient. Before I could say anything, though, he said, "You know, Kenny, last week some employee sent me a bunch of flowers, thanking me for something I did. I'm not even sure who it was, or what I did. But it got me thinking. I only have a few more years before I retire and I think I'd like to use that time focusing on individual employees, their needs and concerns. I know it's impractical—we've got 12,000 of them. But I'd like to give it a try."

Gulp! Now I felt both entrapped and embarrassed. How could I tell him that I sent the flowers—or that he was only part of a program I was testing out? He had arrived at a worthwhile executive goal that I wasn't going to knock off track. I kept my mouth shut, gave my update, and exited as fast as I could.

These two conversations made me want to continue my plans with the Mr. Hatch award. I believed Bob would support the plan. The pilot even taught me a few lessons: run the program on my own and forget about formal corporate support; keep the anonymity of the program intact; ditch the corporate florist.

The next Monday, I moved into full implementation. I chose two more workers, but didn't go to the swanky florist. I walked a few blocks north into downtown Brooklyn and found an all-purpose store. The proprietor sells a lot of things, including flowers. I said to him, "Here's my offer. Every week I want you to deliver two floral arrangements to our headquarters. I also want a "thank you" balloon attached along with a note that I'll give you. You put the note in an envelope and deliver it all. I'll pay cash. You don't contact me; I only contact you. I'll show up every Monday with the names, notes, and money."

Unlike the corporate florist, he had no problem with this arrangement. Apparently he does a lot of his business this way. "One final question," I said. "What kind of flowers do I get for my $40?" "Give me a minute," he replied. What he brought back was a massive array of floral specimens: birds of paradise, tulips, roses, Baby's-breath. I think I got half of his storefront display. "Looks fine to me," I nodded. "Do a good job, and I'll keep coming back every week."

I'm still sending flowers, anonymous notes, and balloons. With the exception of Bob, nobody knows anything about it. Mr. Hatch and I haven't revolutionized KeySpan's corporate culture. Yet some things are a little different. For starters, I actually look forward to coming to work on Monday mornings and seldom if ever think about my own mortality. In addition, a small number of employees go home Monday night with a smile or quizzical look on their faces.

I've also discovered that co-workers have had a blast trying to figure out who is sending flowers to their friends and why. I suspect a few even dream of receiving flowers and balloons for themselves. I've also witnessed the executive I had been working with making retirement plans by meeting individually with employees. And lastly, I've got a proprietor in downtown Brooklyn who smiles when he sees me coming and warmly shakes my hand.

Mr. Hatch serves as a living reminder to me about the need to reward employees not only for what they do, but more importantly, for who they are. It is the oft-hidden qualities of employee character and integrity that make the company special. I am always encouraged when I think of the intrinsic value of people and how important it is to nurture that value in a multitude of informal ways. The events of September 11th would be a further reminder of the depths of this truth.

CHAPTER EIGHT

September 11th

I am not resigned to the shutting away of loving hearts in the hard ground.

—Edna St. Vincent Millay

On the morning of September 11, 2001, Kenny Moore arrived at Boston's Logan Airport at 7:30. He and Craig Matthews had flown in from Newark Airport and were scheduled to hold a meeting with a group of New England employees at the company's West Roxbury facility. As they left Logan in a hired car, they had no idea that at that moment, two groups of hijackers had just boarded flights at Logan terminals, intent on a mission that would transcend reason and ignite a shocking and tragic chain of events.

Out on Long Island, Bob Catell left his home in Garden City and made the short trip to KeySpan's Hicksville offices. At 8 A.M., he convened a meeting of nearly all of KeySpan's officers at which Gerry Luterman, chief financial officer, was to discuss the 2002 budget.

At MetroTech, KeySpan's headquarters in Brooklyn, people were streaming into the building, reluctant to move inside from the faultless late summer morning. From the windows of KeySpan, the panoramic view across the East River was breathtaking, even to longtime employees, who never grew tired of the sight. An azure sky

framed the magnificent Manhattan skyline. The Empire State Building at midtown and the twin towers of the World Trade Center directly across from MetroTech glinted in the morning sun. The air
was so clear and pristine that the cityscape seemed unreal, like a
movie backdrop.

When the first plane, American Airlines Flight 11, crashed into
the north tower of the World Trade Center at 8:46 A.M., the massive explosion showered the streets with glass and debris. Few
KeySpan employees had seen anything from their vantage point,
but word spread quickly around MetroTech as a giant plume of
black smoke and visible fire were seen amid the falling wreckage.
Shocked employees rushed to the windows overlooking the catastrophe. They believed they were looking at the aftermath of a horrible accident.

In Hicksville, Catell's executive assistant, Virginia, entered the
meeting room and quietly handed Catell a note. It said simply that a
plane had crashed into the World Trade Center. Also thinking that a
terrible accident had occurred, Catell told the group what he had
learned and excused himself to go to his office, where he had a television. As he stood watching the live pictures of the devastating scene,
the second plane, United Air Lines Flight 175, slammed into the
south tower with stunning impact.

The moment was dizzying, incredible. Like everyone else witnessing the event, Catell knew immediately that this was not an accident
at all. He felt a flash of fear mixed with anguish. He thought about the
horror of the people on the planes and in the twin towers. He thought
about his family and where they were at that moment. He realized
that his brother-in-law worked on the 58th floor of one of the towers.
He then thought about his people at MetroTech, directly across the
river. Like everyone else, he understood on a visceral level that a catastrophe of unimaginable proportions was underway. He also felt the
immediate weight of his leadership role and that much had to be
done, and quickly. He sprinted back to the meeting room and informed his officers about what had happened, setting in motion a
checklist of actions that must be taken. The officers had heard the

news and were reaching for their cell phones. Catell told everyone to make sure KeySpan facilities were secure and that the massive energy-generating plants posed no danger to the public. He urged them to check on their people as best they could.

On a day when leaders would be desperately needed, nearly all of the company's officers were away from headquarters. Catell phoned his wife, who was trying to remain calm but was growing upset at the thought of her sister's husband in the towers. No one had yet heard from him. Catell urged her to go to her sister's house to be with her as they awaited news. He then called MetroTech, trying to make sure that the people at KeySpan were protected. With events unfolding on a television screen and chaos and panic beginning to spread around lower Manhattan, Catell knew he would have trouble getting into Brooklyn. It was the most helpless he'd ever felt.

Inside MetroTech, employees had gathered at the windows and witnessed the horror of the second plane crashing into the south tower. Around the building, screams and cries of agony could be heard. Televisions had been turned on in conference rooms, and news reports mentioned several more planes unaccounted for and possibly hijacked as well. A mounting hysteria spread throughout the building. If the country was under attack and New York City was a major target, where could they go to find safety? From their vantage point, some employees saw people leaping from the towers as the flames and smoke funneled out of both buildings. Several KeySpan people passed out; others were sobbing and terrified. Many wanted to get out of the tall building, leave MetroTech and rush home, but the city's transportation system was in disarray and the streets were filling with crowds in a growing panic.

Suddenly, the first tower began to collapse and send a terrifying wall of noise and debris cascading down onto the city below. Soon thereafter, the second tower fell and transformed lower Manhattan into what felt and looked like a bombed-out war zone. As it did all over New York and the world, the horror of the images created widespread panic and terror inside MetroTech. The scenes from lower Manhattan were surreal: people running for their lives covered with a layer of gray soot with a blossoming cloud of debris emerging from the wreckage, chasing them down the city's streets.

Bob Catell managed to reach supervisors at MetroTech and sent them from floor to floor to try to calm the now nearly hysterical employee population. Essential personnel were asked to stay at their posts, and others were told they could leave if they wanted to but were advised that the roads were closed all over the city and the subway system was nearly paralyzed. Employees who did leave the building later that day encountered the ghostly parade of thousands covered with gray dust, many injured and bleeding, as they moved in eerie silence over the Brooklyn Bridge away from the catastrophe and onto Flatbush Avenue in Brooklyn.

Cheryl Smith, then KeySpan's senior vice president and chief information officer, lived in Battery Park, directly across from the World Trade Center. She was working at her home office that morning when the first plane hit. She grabbed a pair of sandals, left her apartment, and then watched in horror as the morning events unfolded. When the towers began to collapse, she ran for her life, eventually making her way to the waterfront near the Brooklyn Bridge.

"I remember eventually getting to the water but it seemed like a complete dead end and I turned back to go somewhere else," Smith said. "I decided that I needed to get to Brooklyn so I started up the ramp that winds into the entrance of the bridge. I realized that I had hurt my knee by then so it was somewhat slow going and I kept thinking, one more step. When we got to the middle of the Brooklyn Bridge I think that we all realized that we were going to make it. It was such an incredible relief. The world was light again; it was actually a beautiful day. We were covered in filth and some were hurt and limping or burned or bleeding or were being helped by friends, but everyone knew that God was not going to take us that day."

Other KeySpan employees had indelible experiences. "We returned to our units where we received our assignments," said Joseph Drucker, a member of a KeySpan crew that went to lower Manhattan. "We mostly cut off active services right by Ground Zero to buildings that were once full of life, but were now abandoned."

"We raced onto the first ferry to help the injured and stood in the middle of the boat as people walked off covered with dust," said Frank Marino, a KeySpan worker on Staten Island. "There was only one minor injury and that's when we realized how bad the situation was."

"During this tragedy, I saw everyone at MetroTech come together in support of each other in a matter of seconds," said Deane Moore, a KeySpan employee visiting from Massachusetts. "No words can adequately describe the unity and brotherhood that were exhibited by all."

In Boston, Kenny Moore was climbing into a company car with Craig Matthews to head back to New York. Matthews had immediately canceled the meeting, and when every plane in the United States was grounded they decided to drive back. On the ride, news reports made it clear that they were not going to get back into the city. They headed instead to their homes in New Jersey. Moore tried to contact Catell but could not reach him. As he confronted the momentous events of that day, he knew that something fundamental had shifted in the world and that he would soon face a massive new challenge in his life. Coming just months after his open-heart surgery, the tragedy caused him to sense the unmistakable presence of death, and he worried whether he was physically capable of taking on this challenge. What people were experiencing was unlike anything that had happened in history, so to prepare for its aftermath was impossible. Undoubtedly, it would be very hard and take a very long time.

For Catell, the events unfolded with a chilling clarity that something ominous and unknown had been unleashed in the United States that day. Like other business leaders in New York, Catell reached out to companies that were suffering perhaps more than KeySpan. Though he couldn't be certain of anything on that first day, Catell believed that no one from KeySpan had been killed in the World Trade Center. He was fairly certain, however, that many employees had lost loved ones that day. His family had been spared when they heard from his brother-in-law earlier in the day. He had been at his desk when the first plane hit. He had walked down all 58 floors and escaped just minutes before the tower collapsed.

Catell had contacted Gene McGrath, his counterpart at Con Edison in Manhattan. He knew that Con Ed would be devastated by the attack, and he offered any and all assistance in the coming days and weeks. He also met with Richard Kessel, the chairman of LIPA, who came over to Hicksville to monitor the day's events. Once it became clear that the company's generating facilities were secure and further attacks were hopefully not imminent, Catell felt fortunate and thankful.

He sent out a short e-mail to all employees, knowing that many had stayed at their desks despite the attack. He knew no words could suffice, but he felt that he had to communicate.

Today's terrorist attacks against New York City and our country are impossible for us to comprehend. Our thoughts, our prayers, and our support go out to the victims and their families and friends. I know that many employees witnessed this horrific event from our MetroTech building and were deeply affected by the sight. To be so close to such senseless devastation undermines our sense of security and well-being. I encourage you to talk to each other about your feelings, and to use the services of our counselors, to help work through the very natural emotional distress you may be experiencing. It will take time and our collective strength to come to terms with this tragedy. We will get through it together, as a company and a country.

Unlike some companies, KeySpan had a track record for responding to disasters. Not only did it handle emergencies within its own territory, but KeySpan employees were ready to mobilize to offer assistance in earthquakes, hurricanes, or floods in other states or countries. Though the magnitude of this day was unparalleled, Catell believed that his people would recover enough to respond as they always had to a crisis. Their hearts would not allow them to do anything else.

In one of his many extracurricular activities, Catell served as chairman of the New York City Partnership, a Manhattan-based nonprofit organization made up of 200 CEOs of the city's top businesses. The Partnership's mandate was to enhance the economy and maintain New York City's position as the global center of commerce, culture, and innovation. Catell called Kathy Wylde, the president of the group, to offer his assistance and make sure the staff, based in lower Manhattan, was all right.

After a number of his officers tried unsuccessfully to get back into the city that day, Catell stayed at Hicksville until late into the night. He made arrangements to get into MetroTech early the next morning and then headed home to his wife Joan. The entirety of the day overcame him as he hugged her for a long time. The sense of fear, the disbelief, and the enormity of what had happened and what was still unfolding all came together in one emotional moment. What would happen tomorrow and in the days to come seemed incalculable, but he knew that a lot of people would be looking to him for direction, comfort, and stability. That night, he prayed for the strength he would need to confront this massive new and unknowable challenge. And he resolved that one of the first people he would call when he arrived in Brooklyn was Kenny Moore.

The CEO

~

When I arrived at my office at MetroTech on the morning of September 12, I stared out at a scene that I will remember the rest of my life. For 10 years, ever since we had moved the company into this building and I became CEO, I had looked out upon a stunning view of lower Manhattan and the majestic twin towers of the World Trade Center. On this morning, there was a giant hole in the horizon, an empty space surrounded by gray smoke and the painfully inadequate skyline that remained.

The feeling in the pit of my stomach was indescribable. I couldn't believe that this nightmare was actually real. In fact, until that moment when I actually got to witness that emptiness, I guess I hadn't really been able to comprehend what had happened. Many months later, I still catch myself when I arrive in the morning feeling a quick sense of expectation that the towers will still be there.

That first morning and for a few days afterward, I tried to put my emotions in check and become the leader the company needed at that moment. Whatever I was feeling personally, I knew that I had to maintain my composure as best as I could and give people a sense that I had control of the situation, at least as far as KeySpan was concerned. I met with Kenny Moore to get his sage advice as to how to handle this wrenching situation. After years of working together, I felt that now was the time I needed Kenny's counsel more than ever. We had always had an unspoken agreement to keep religion out of our conversations. But this felt different, and having someone with Kenny's background brought me a level of comfort that his advice would be appropriate and tinged with divine inspiration.

At Kenny's suggestion, I went from floor to floor to reach out to every single employee. I felt that I had to touch as many people as I could, literally touch them and put my arms around them and let them know that I was there for them. People cried on my shoulder. I cried with them. They were visibly shaken. I asked each one if they were okay, whether they had lost anyone in the collapse of the towers. I learned that a number of our employees—55 as it turned out—had lost loved ones. It was undoubtedly the most emotional experience I've had in my professional life.

I knew that there were thousands of other KeySpan employees suffering the deep emotion of this catastrophe. But the people at MetroTech had endured a significant trauma, having witnessed the event from the windows of our building, seeing the horror as closely as they had. One young man, perhaps in his midtwenties, came up to me. He was shaking, obviously traumatized. I put my arm around his shoulder, and he said, "Mr. Catell, I love working for KeySpan, but I just can't work in a tall building anymore. I just can't work here anymore." I tried to console him, calm him down. I told him that he should do what he had to do. I hoped he would change his mind after he had time to deal with the trauma.

I spoke to Elaine Weinstein and made sure that we had grief counselors on site as quickly as possible. I sensed that people appreciated having me walk around, so I continued. It took me three days to visit everyone. During that time, we were learning more details about what had happened. And we were learning, yet again, how the people of KeySpan react to crisis.

Before I could ask anyone to do anything, our people were down at Ground Zero volunteering to help in any way they could. Our operations people sent crews to lower Manhattan to help Con Edison turn off gas mains and deal with downed electrical power operations. Our employees gave blood, clothes, and materials, and opened their homes to people who couldn't get back to their homes in lower Manhattan. With the giving spirit they had always displayed, they embraced the widespread need that blanketed New York City. We set up a matching gift program for employee donations to various relief efforts, which quickly surpassed $1 million. I wasn't surprised, but I was profoundly moved.

I met again with Kenny to discuss what we should do about our people. When I started to hear about employees who had lost loved ones, I wasn't sure how best to handle the situation. I thought to call each one personally, but I worried that I was imposing on them in a time of unspeakable grief. But Kenny convinced me that it would be the right thing to do.

I have often called people directly to congratulate them for some work well done. I've found that the response to a personal call is remarkable; people feel not only gratitude but a sense of great pride to have the CEO take time to speak with them. Kenny alerted me that these calls would not be anything like that. He understood that engineers have a great need to fix things, solve problems, provide a remedy. But that was not going to happen here.

Kenny told me to simply acknowledge their pain and let it be. He told me that just listening would be a great gift, and he was right. As I started making these calls and hearing the anguish and the grief, I realized that I could do only one or two of these calls at a time. I wanted to be able to listen, stay with them for a while, and be sensitive to their needs. I scheduled these calls in a way that I would not be interrupted, which was difficult under the circumstances. Very often after our conversation I would receive e-mails or personal notes of thanks, and I forwarded those to Kenny so that he could follow up and offer assistance.

I knew that we would need to do more as time passed. Speaking with Kenny, I understood there were no business solutions to any of this. If ever corporate America needed a spiritual embrace, this was the time. For weeks after the tragedy, the sense of shock and a free-floating anxiety permeated our offices, as it did all over the city and the country. In early November, an airliner crashed in the Belle Harbor section of Rockaway, Queens, near Kennedy Airport, sending already frayed nerves to the breaking point. It turned out that it was not another terrorist act but it was a horrible tragedy nonetheless. Belle Harbor had just lost a staggering number of its residents, firefighters and others, in the 9/11 tragedy.

We had work crews in the neighborhood at the time of the crash and they had to run for their lives as a giant fireball incinerated a city block. Two of our workers, seeing an elderly couple trapped in their homes, raced in and rescued them. They told me later they were just doing their jobs, but the couple said, "These weren't workers, they were guardian angels." Sometimes commerce intersects with real life in unexpected, utterly noncommercial ways. Sometimes that intersection is the place where spirituality and destiny come together and cannot be explained by our rational everyday thoughts. Being a company that was so tied into the community, we experienced this tragic time in a very personal way. Most of those firefighters and police officers who perished in the twin towers were from the neighborhoods we served, and we felt a deep kinship to them and to their families.

There are many memories from that time that remain vivid for me. On a Sunday morning about two months after 9/11, I was going to a meeting of the New York City Partnership in lower Manhattan. We were meeting with Senators Charles Schumer and Hillary Clinton to talk about getting funds to New York City to begin restoration. I was near Ground Zero and had stopped to show my identification to police officers at the barricades. A memorial service for relatives of victims was going to take place later that morning, so there was a huge crowd of people converging on the area. I felt a tap on my shoulder.

When I turned, I saw a beautiful young woman named Rosaleen Shea who had once worked for KeySpan. She had lost her sister in the tragedy and I had heard about it and telephoned to offer my condolences. And here, in the midst of thousands of people, she had spotted me in the crowd. Without a word, we embraced and we both started crying. I don't know why or how we had come together in that place on that day. But all the emotion of the previous weeks finally just overwhelmed me and came flooding out. She thanked me for reaching out to her. I told her again how sorry I was about her sister. I don't know how you figure out why things happen in this world, but that unexpected encounter certainly made me feel as if there was a greater power up there somewhere that orchestrates these sacred moments in each of our lives.

Kenny suggested that we should do something in a public way to acknowledge the losses suffered on 9/11. But he also advised me to wait and allow a period of grieving. The holidays were coming up and we knew this would be the hardest time for everyone who had been touched by the tragedy. So we decided to do a memorial service in January.

I had mixed emotions about this as well. Again, there was a sense that we were imposing on people's grief. Kenny convinced me, though, that this would be a good thing to do if we waited until January. I agreed. But I insisted this be done discreetly and in good taste. I didn't want this to be a media event. There would be no press, no pictures, not even coverage in the company newsletter. The people who had lost loved ones would be invited, along with their family members. We would invite only corporate officers in whose groups these people worked. Kenny recommended that we hold the memorial away from KeySpan and suggested a beautiful setting, the Palm House in the Brooklyn Botanic Gardens.

He orchestrated a very moving ceremony, not religious in the sense of prayers and biblical readings but sensitive and supportive. I welcomed everyone and thanked them for coming. A choral group from KeySpan performed. Elaine Weinstein read a poem by Elizabeth Barrett Browning and then spoke about the resources available from HR for those who were grieving. Kenny also brought poetry and even children's literature to the service. He read from *The Velveteen Rabbit* by Margery Williams.

I asked if any of the family members wanted to say something. The room was quiet for several moments until one man stood up and talked with tears in his eyes about his brother. Another person read a poem about her sister. Nearly every family member stood and said something through their tears and anguish. The sound of sobbing permeated the room. It was a transcendent experience, completely unscripted but deeply moving. There are truly no words to effectively describe the emotion of that day. Those who were there, including myself, will likely never forget it. Kenny and I received a note afterward from Steven Vitale, a KeySpan vice president who attended the ceremony.

> Thank you for yet another act of greatness. What you did today for those who lost loved ones in the 9/11 tragedy will be fondly remembered. It is this that makes KeySpan different and a special place to work. I know I speak for many when I convey this message of thanks.

Kenny had the idea that people should take away something with them, something symbolic. The 100-year garden, a stand of beautiful oaks that had grown for 100 years, was due that spring to be replaced for the next century. We spoke about plans to start a memorial tree garden here at the Botanic Gardens in which a scarlet oak would be the first new oak planted in the spring in remembrance of lost loved ones. I called each family member up to the podium, read off the name of their lost loved one, and gave them a stained glass oak leaf that Kenny had had made up for the occasion. After thanking everyone for coming and wishing them the strength to cope with their loss, I invited them all to join me for a luncheon that Kenny had arranged. I felt emotionally spent. Months had elapsed since 9/11 but the weight had hardly lessened at all. In some ways, it never would.

For someone who had never been a particularly emotional person, I was experiencing all this in an extremely personal way. Like others, I felt violated. This was my city, these were my neighbors, my customers, my employees. There was a hurt and anger I had never experienced before. It was close to the surface and I had to remind myself over and over that we had a responsibility to get back to work, to make sure that life would go on.

I'm not sure any of us can ever fully get over what happened on September 11th. I still meet people who remind me that I walked around the building comforting our employees who had witnessed the tragedy and I can still feel their emotional scars. But being the kind of company we are, and having the responsibility to serve the public, we had to keep the business running and move forward. To me, it was the blessing of democratic capitalism that we have this freedom to make something of our lives and, if we are lucky, touch other lives at the same time. It was a powerful reminder of why this was all so important to me in the first place.

The Monk

~

I've come to notice that the way our employees show up in work is the same way they show up in the world. While I've always been impressed with the dedication they bring to their jobs and to their commitment to the world around them, I was singularly struck by the valor they demonstrated on September 11th. The ancient Greeks used to say that adversity reveals greatness while prosperity merely masks it.

We live and work with people, often believing them to be ordinary. Then tragedy strikes, and suddenly our co-workers rise to the occasion, risking their own safety, getting involved, making amazing choices. That day and in the days that followed, we witnessed many ordinary employees behaving in extraordinary ways. The greatness demonstrated in the face of this catastrophe came from a place deep within their hearts and souls. I had daily witnessed their selflessness in the workplace and was honored to see it so quickly flow out into the community when that fateful day arrived.

The trauma and vulnerability that I personally experienced from my heart attack in January was felt collectively by the nation in September. When confronted with the mystery of evil in the world, we are all left with more questions than answers.

"When death makes its unwelcome visit to the workplace, there's no response you can offer to diminish the horror," I told Bob as we talked together after the twin towers fell. I reminded him that his greatest gift at that moment was to remain publicly visible before the employees. "Forget about speaking words of hope to them. You literally need to *be* hope for them."

As I ministered to the many employees traumatized by this event,

I was reminded of the quote of Saint John of the Cross that hung in the monastery chapel: "And I saw a river over which every soul must pass to reach the kingdom of heaven and the name of that river was 'suffering' . . . and then I saw a boat which carries souls across the river and the name of that boat was 'love.' "

I came to learn that being present with our employees during this unsettling time was enough. "I appreciate you just listening to me rant and rave," one engineer told me. "I apologize for getting so upset. But I just needed someone who would be there and not judge or try to give me answers."

In times of loss, our best offering is not in being strong with others, but in being weak with them. It's not always about "doing" something. Often it's more about "being" with someone. Learning to just keep myself quiet and be with distraught workers was sufficient. Our more precious gifts come from somewhere inside us that is vulnerable, weak, and deficient. I occasionally wondered in offering my personal poverty whether it would be of much value. I came to see that it was the most restorative potion any human being could give.

Bringing employees together, offering a listening ear and accepting the broad swath of raging emotions that spew forth in the face of injustice also helped employees heal and move forward. Tragedy even had some unintended consequences, as one union worker reminded me: "I didn't realize how much I'd taken life for granted," he told me. "It makes me feel both angry and thankful at the same time."

After the terrorist attack, I noticed an increase in the number of prayer cards and inspirational notes on the desks and workstations of employees. I saw missives to the Divine: a prayer for serenity; a blessing for a loved one; a spiritual thought for a departed friend. They stand as a reminder that life is sacred and it's not necessary to be in church or synagogue to remember this. The workplace has proved to be more than an adequate venue for this spiritual reflection. Tragic events are always an invitation to deepen our interior life and seek a source of security beyond the human. Money, promotions, and corporate perks can't provide that. A deep interior life can.

On September 11th, employees defined their values by the actions they took. Business and profit took a backseat to family and loved ones. Things that were taken for granted reemerged as priorities. In an age of high-tech machinery, people longed for the warmth of the human touch and the sound of a person's voice. People sought comfort in community. For some, it was their religious organizations or neighborhood associations. For many others, it was the workplace. That is where community was sought, nurtured, and, if necessary, created.

Healing and reconciliation would take place where people labored. Business, more than religion or politics, remains the world's dominant community. It's where most of the people work out their lives, their vocations, and their destiny. We live and die in contact with the workplace and the employees who inhabit it. We have come to look to it not only for economic sustenance, but also for personal and moral sustenance as well.

As a company, we were accustomed to recognizing and celebrating the achievements of our employees. In hosting the memorial service to commemorate family members lost that day, we found ourselves in another domain. As Bob and I prepared for the ceremony, we both understood this. "I want this to be an opportunity for them to share their thoughts and feelings," he said. "While the ceremony can't be religious, I think it needs to be sacred."

Choosing to host the memorial service at a botanic garden offered us a reminder of the cycle of life. The bareness of winter would eventually give way to the rebirth of spring. The ceremony would celebrate the lives of those no longer with us, and would allow us to gather strength from one another.

As the sun shone through the glass-enclosed room, Bob welcomed the employees and their families: "Your presence here today says we feel there is strength in being together." It was hard to know what to do and say in circumstances like this. He reminded them: "Tragic events present us with situations that we cannot comprehend and for which we cannot prepare. Management books do not have a chapter for times like this."

One of the readings I selected for the event was from Margery Williams' *The Velveteen Rabbit*, a children's story about a toy animal's journey in becoming real. Profound truths often are captured in children's literature.

"What is Real?" asks the Rabbit of the wise Skin Horse, the only other nursery toy to successfully make the transition from plaything to real. "Does it mean having things that buzz inside you and a stick-out handle?"

The Skin Horse responds that becoming real isn't about appearances or successes. It's about the giving and receiving of love. "Generally, by the time you are Real," he says, "most of your hair has been loved off, and your eyes drop out and you get loose in the joints and very shabby. But these things don't matter at all, because once you are Real you can't be ugly, except to people who don't understand."

What this group and all who were touched by the tragedy endured made them feel shabby and ragged. But an unintended consequence of tragedy is that we emerge in a different place, sometimes a more humane place with the potential to deepen our compassion as human beings.

I purposely designed into the program a period of time for the employees to publicly share their distress and hope. Many spoke poignantly about their losses. Several took the opportunity to share the depth of their despair as well as the mystery of their sacred journey.

"Many days I feel like I can no longer go on," one employee shared with the group. "But that's not what my brother would have wanted. I've come to see that I need to be strong—not only for myself, but also for him." Tears, grief, forgiveness, and compassion filled the garden room that morning.

Afterward, several employees wrote me letters of thanks. Said one attendee: "Thank you for including us in the Memorial Service. It meant so much to me and especially my Dad. The music, the readings, and allowing us to share our memories (and yes, our grief as well) are a tribute to you and your courage to do this for us." She seemed to also take away a deeper message: "As you read the excerpt from *The Velveteen Rabbit*, I was left with a renewed hope to embrace my life and my loves as deeply as before—the pain is as real as my love for my sister."

Many more letters came to Bob. Some employees needed several months to elapse before they were able to extend their gratitude. "It's been six months since my sister passed away. I just wanted to let you know how grateful I am for everything you and all of KeySpan have done for me." While it would take much time, our employees as well as our nation would heal from this wound and strengthen the resolve required for moving forward.

While sitting in my office on November 12, I saw a vast plume of smoke rise from my corner window. The crash of an American Airlines flight outside Kennedy Airport was visible to all of us. As we anxiously held our collective breath, I left my office and went floor to floor meeting with employees, offering support, getting other managers to do the same thing.

After we found out that this was not another terrorist attack, the mood calmed down a bit. That day, a group of Girl Scouts were in our lobby selling cookies for their annual fund-raiser. I went over and bought a few dozen boxes and proceeded to go from floor to floor offering them to employees. "Please take one," I'd say. "It's just a small token of appreciation for all you offer the company." I invited them to keep an eye on their fellow workers and notify me in the event that some employees became distressed or anxious.

While there were many practical things that I did on that day, possibly the most significant and worthwhile was in the offering of the cookies. It served as a small token of communion, appreciation, and normalcy. It also reminded me that we were not just a place of employment. We were also a community of people.

CHAPTER NINE

~

Preserving the
Corporate Goodness

We must be the change we wish to see in the world.

—Mahatma Gandhi

At 6:30, on a chilly late October morning in 2002, Bob Catell arrives at KeySpan's Court Street Field Operations Center in the Red Hook section of Brooklyn. It is still dark outside when he enters the building in this ramshackle waterfront neighborhood. Awaiting Catell's arrival are 30 to 40 operations personnel, union workers who make up the field crews that are a familiar sight on the streets of Brooklyn. Also waiting is Kenny Moore and a small group of supervisors and vice presidents.

The workers, clad in Yankees, Mets, Jets, or New York Giants caps, jeans, and KeySpan sweatshirts, are bleary-eyed and make their way to the free coffee and pastry, chatting in thick Brooklyn accents about football and plans for the upcoming weekend. Catell, in his ever present suit, tie, and wingtips, enters the tiny cafeteria, shaking hands, greeting old acquaintances by their first names, introducing himself to new faces as if he were just another company worker. A story that circulates around KeySpan is that Catell, even as CEO with his 45 years of service, always shows his employee ID badge when entering a company facility. It simply doesn't occur to him to be treated differently from other employees. Here, he is smiling and comfortable in a setting that is familiar and nostalgic. The first 15 years of his career were in distribution and operations.

The visit to Red Hook is one of Catell's periodic field visits to locations all around KeySpan, from Brooklyn to Staten Island to Long Island to Boston. As the company has grown, Catell has felt increased frustration at his inability to connect with more employees, but he has never ceased to make the effort. He understands that the culture he has so carefully nurtured over the years must be constantly tended and proliferated to new parts of the organization. He has read countless books on business theory and knows that most mergers fail because of cultural dysfunction. Four years into the LILCO merger and two into the Eastern acquisition, Catell is determined that the KeySpan story will not be yet another case study of a failed coupling.

But Catell is aware that both he and the company are at a crossroads. Though the board has extended his contract for two more years, he is beginning to embrace the reality of impending retirement. Finding a successor is a high priority, a task made more challenging by the uncertain business climate that has settled on the industry like a stationary storm front. The bleak economic outlook is threatening to taint Catell's legacy. Rather than walk off into a glorious sunset with violins at a crescendo, Catell worries that the near-term picture may make for a gloomy, unsatisfying ending. This cuts against the grain of a man who believes that those who do good works reap the rewards.

At the same time, Catell is an unapologetic optimist, genetically incapable of dwelling on the negative. In more than four decades of professional experience, he has witnessed the endless up and down cycles of business that move like sine waves across time. Every trough feels unrelenting, but inevitably upturns occur. Engineers can't get locked into corners, because there is always a solution, no matter how daunting the problem.

In the bowels of the operations center, Catell addresses the union workers, who are seated in folding chairs in front of him. He greets them with his usual offer of thanks, telling them that it is the people who make the company what it is. Though Catell believes this deeply, the blue-collar workforce tends to be cynical, and body language makes clear that not everyone is moved by Catell's sincerity. Employees, both union and nonunion, have heard rumblings about coming cost containment and potential head count reductions. In the midst of a horrible economy, such news tends to undermine morale and increase anxiety levels around the company. But Catell strongly believes that the good news still outweighs the bad for KeySpan, and though he doesn't sugarcoat the problems, he remains upbeat about the future.

Noting the frosty morning—"good gas company weather"—he recommends that everyone join him in wishing for a long, cold winter, unlike the previous one, which set records for high temperatures. Cognizant that these employees are also shareholders, Catell offers a synopsis of the company's fiscal outlook and explains why keeping costs in line was becoming a priority in the months ahead. Unlike in times past, these workers are savvy investors who track the stock market and its impact on their 401(k) plans. Catell understands that and speaks as he would to a group of financial analysts, explaining price/earnings ratios, stock valuations, and the need to keep paying a solid dividend. He tells everyone to diversify their stock holdings—not to put all their eggs in the KeySpan basket, despite the stock's relatively stable performance in an otherwise bleak market.

Opening up the floor, Catell fields some tough questions about layoffs, opportunities for advancement within the operations group, 401(k) plans, and diversity. Union workers tend to be bolder in challenging authority and offer up a string of questions and concerns about various issues. Several press Catell for better answers. "I don't see a diverse workforce," says one worker. "I don't see progress there."

Catell is not flustered by the assertion. He nods and assures the man that not only is diversity a high priority but his officers' compensation is tied to their handling of this issue. He agrees that things have not moved as quickly as he would like but that the company has made a strong commitment in this area and it is an issue that he personally tends to. Another questioner complains about a lack of opportunity for upward career mobility. Yet another points out a glitch in resolving a customer's heating problems that took six days to fix.

Employee complaints are nothing new for Catell. Union workers may be more outspoken, but Catell has been sensing more discontent in his visits with management workers as well. In a company of 12,000 employees, some will always view the job as just a paycheck, a place to put in their time. There will always be complaints. But Catell has felt a shift. Those longing for the good old days, for the cozy, familial feelings of Brooklyn Union Gas, are being confronted by the anxieties of this new millennium work environment. Tenets of decades past—loyalty, longevity, commitment, spirit, and a sense of family—are all still evident at KeySpan. But Catell senses it is getting harder to sustain such feelings, to instill a creed that had become suspect in this complex and tense political and economic climate.

He didn't satisfy everybody that morning at Red Hook, but he managed to close the meeting on an upbeat note and make his way out of the building shaking hands and sharing congenial moments with veteran workers whom he had known for years. He left the building as he had entered, smiling.

Kenny Moore watched the entire encounter and believed it went well. Both his monastic life and his business experience have taught him that people's complaints are not only inevitable, but encouraging. He points out that most people believe the opposite of love is hate. But in monastic principle, the opposite of love is not hate but apathy. The fact that someone hates and complains implies that they still have energy and passion for the relationship. When the complaining stops, it signals indifference, a lack of caring any longer. That is the time to start worrying. "I take heart when I go into a room with employees who are angry and complain," he says. "It means they care."

Within the province of business, however, caring is an ethereal concept. Even as Catell prepares for the end of a long and productive career, he continues to care deeply about every aspect of his company. He also acknowledges that the current business environment is far more fractured and difficult than it was 15 years ago. So not only inviting but receiving the same deep commitment back from employees today is a challenging, increasingly problematic, occasionally impossible task. If he cannot find a way to preserve the core goodness and values of the company, few are going to care as much as he does.

The winter of 2002–2003 turned out to be colder, snowier, and more intense than Catell could have hoped for. Buoyed by a dramatic increase in gas usage and several favorable one-time charges, the fiscal year ended on a high note, with record revenues and earnings. Nonetheless, financial pressures increased, and what might have been cause to celebrate got lost in a gathering rush to tighten budgets, slash costs, and reduce head count.

KeySpan found itself in a sort of fiscal netherworld while the dismal economic news continued unabated. Never perceived as a high-flying growth company, KeySpan was solid and stable, recession-resistant as long as people needed to turn on their heat and their lights. It is a company that has paid a dividend for more than 100 years and one of the few in the energy field to enjoy an excellent credit rating. Catell has spent more hours than he can recount figuring out ways to convince the marketplace that KeySpan remains a good place in which to invest.

But coming on the heels of 9/11 and facing current economic conditions, shareholders wanted to know where the company was headed. There were no easy answers. Catell could steer a steady course of business as usual and find ways to grow the core gas and electric businesses by 6 to 8 percent annually. He could search for new acquisition candidates in order to grow the company dramatically. Or he could consider offers that might be beneficial to shareholders, such as a mega-merger with cross-river rival Con Edison. His preference was to stay the course and search for new buying opportunities. He wanted to stay focused in the Northeast and found a limited number of enticing candidates. Nonetheless, his phone rang constantly with calls from investment bankers armed with deals.

At the same time, Catell worried about preserving the corporate goodness that had emerged from Brooklyn Union. Saving the company but losing its soul would be a sad, empty legacy to leave behind, and he desperately sought a way to avoid such a fate.

Throughout the fall and winter, Catell and his officers conducted meetings at the company's locations trumpeting the need for cost containment. Though he promised no layoffs, Catell acknowledged that there would be performance-related terminations. The response was uniform around the company as a malaise of gloom settled in. Catell was puzzled, but he shouldn't have been. In a utility some people tend to have a civil service attitude, and to them the idea of performance rating was inconceivable. For some who put in 20 or more years with the company, there was a feeling of entitlement: "I've put in my time. Now is the time to coast, and nobody is going to touch me." When someone like that gets tapped on the shoulder and is asked to pack up their office, there is inevitably bitterness and resentment.

Catell believed that a layoff meant an across-the-board cutback— 10 percent, 20 percent, or 30 percent across every department. Targeted cost reductions, he felt, were simply not the same thing. But the feeling among the troops was that it was just a matter of semantics; however one defined workforce reductions, it meant people losing their jobs. If it walked like a duck and squawked like a duck, you could name it whatever you wanted, but it was still a duck.

Moore met with Catell several times throughout the winter to relay this message. What he was hearing out on the front lines was a growing discontent and alarm. After a few of these meetings, Catell grew testy, annoyed that people didn't seem to be hearing what he was saying. He could not understand why people were immediately embracing the worst-case scenario. Sure, the economy was bad and KeySpan had to tighten its belt. But compared to other industries like the airlines or high tech, where tens of thousands of jobs were cut at a clip, KeySpan faced just a few hundred job cuts, perhaps even less. No one likes to see anyone lose a job, but in a company of more than 12,000 employees the elimination of 200 or 300 unnecessary jobs under these economic conditions did not seem unreasonable.

Catell put his faith in Moore's assessments, though, and listened. Their conversations were calm and direct. Moore had long ago demonstrated that his intuition about the corporate mood was exact.

His tidings had always brought the truth, and his core value lay in his ability to deliver all the information, not just what he perceived the CEO wanted to hear.

As the cutbacks were initiated, the tension inside the company increased. Snafus occurred, and some bitter feelings were unleashed in pockets around the company. Moore told Catell, "I guess we're not good at this, and that's a good thing. It means we've never had the practice before."

Having taken the corporate pulse for several months, Moore then shared his thoughts with Catell and the other corporate officers. In a memo, he noted that he was concerned that the company "may be too singularly focused on financial and operational reductions." He pointed out that while reductions and cost containment measures will likely be a staple for years to come, those subjects cannot be the only corporate conversation that takes place.

He pressed for more focus on the need to engage the creativity and passion of employees rather than just a relentless drumbeat about fiscal restraint:

> I believe that employee passion longs for something more com-pelling and inviting than solely meeting financial goals and achieving cost reductions. We won't be able to "save" our way into prosperity. Likewise, continuing "to do more with less" as well as "coming in earlier and staying later" are only short-term strategies that will eventually demoralize and embitter our em-ployees. As demonstrated on numerous occasions, our employees have the passion and creativity to craft and implement plans and programs and to identify unique opportunities for us to reduce costs, improve performance, enhance services, reenergize morale, and creatively take advantage of deregulation.

It became increasingly apparent to Catell that his remaining time as CEO would be focused on these issues. Philosophically, he consid-ered the question of why the company had to keep getting bigger. If KeySpan could find and sustain 6 to 8 percent growth and its stock price could offer a total return of 10 percent to 12 percent in today's market, what would be the downside of that scenario?

The answer was going to evolve over time. A solution would emerge. He might not be the CEO anymore when it did. But he believed with certainty that he had put the company on the proper course. And perhaps more illuminating was the calm sense of confidence Catell continued to bring to the company even as the tensions flared. He was like a veteran ballplayer coming to bat in the bottom of the ninth inning of a close, crucial game. Even if he didn't slug a home run, those watching felt a confidence that there was no one else they would rather see at the plate at that moment. Catell was, as the saying goes, comfortable in his own skin. A career built on a foundation of integrity and self-discipline can be tremendously satisfying as it winds down.

Characteristically, he never wavered in his commitment to his job and the corporate values. During the Iraq war in the spring of 2003, for example, Catell sent personal notes to the spouses of a dozen employees who had been called to active military duty and sent overseas. Offering appreciation for their service to the country, Catell wrote, "KeySan would like to do something special for the families of those employees on military leave. Perhaps your family would like to attend a Mets game, have a landscaper cut your lawn one week, or enlist the services of a professional cleaning service to do your spring cleaning." This was a small gesture, but one that meant a great deal to the families and said so much about the way the company embraced its people.

During that same time frame, the controversial issue of CEO compensation emerged yet again. Despite a ruinous economy over the past three years and the continuing recession, American CEOs were paid what many felt were obscene amounts of money for their performance. *USA Today* proclaimed, "Bubble hasn't burst yet on CEO salaries despite the times." The *New York Times* declared, "Again, Money Follows the Pinstripes." Even as most CEO compensation packages declined a bit, there were still people like Larry Ellison at

Oracle bringing in $781 million for the year and Dennis Kozlowski of Tyco International receiving $238 million despite dramatic drops in their companies' share prices over the 12-month period.

In an April 2003 *BusinessWeek* executive compensation scorecard, Bob Catell, with his $1.6 million compensation package, was the third *lowest*-paid CEO of the 19 companies in the utilities sector. At the same time, Catell received the highest rating in the sector for pay versus shareholder return over the previous three-year period, the measurement that *BusinessWeek* felt was most indicative of the value a CEO brought to his or her organization.

Catell might have approached his board of directors with those statistics to make a strong argument for a raise. But money had never been his motivating factor, and now, as he began to consider his retirement, he wasn't about to alter his outlook. He was appalled at the behavior of the CEOs who had made headlines over the past 24 months for their greed. But he also resented being painted with the same broad brush, knowing that he and most of his fellow chief executives had not fallen prey to such scandalous conduct. Besides, in his heart he knew he was making far more money than he had ever dreamed he would but it had never affected his lifestyle or his attitude. He and his wife Joan lived in a modest three-bedroom ranch in Garden City. He drove a used Jaguar and derived his pleasure from a round of golf and spending time with his five children and four grandchildren on the weekends.

What impressed most people who met him was that at age 66, Catell showed no inclination to slow down. He was working harder than ever and seemed to be enjoying it as much as he ever had. Perhaps that was why he had not fully embraced the board's desire to focus on management succession. He had to play a significant role in finding his own replacement, a scenario that was already setting off sparks within the organization. Though he knew there were strong candidates both internally and outside the company, some part of Catell just could not imagine walking away.

The CEO

$\mathcal{A}$s Kenny pointed out at our corporate funeral many years ago, you can't begin something new until the past has been properly left behind. Though I still have some time before I retire—and I am certainly not thinking of this as a funeral—I realize that a lot of what I have been doing for the past few years has been preparing for my departure. Leaving behind an organization with which I'll have been intimately involved for more than 47 years is not a simple thing. In fact, though my engineer side has thought through the logistics of finding a successor and making my exit, my emotional side has yet to really grasp the idea of saying good-bye.

But I would be remiss if I didn't leave the past properly behind. Part of that is already completed, at least as much as is humanly possible, because it has been a work in progress ever since I became CEO in 1991. I took the mantle of a company characterized by deeply held values and integrity, and I plan to hand off a company to my successor with those same qualities firmly entrenched.

I remember feeling a tremendous sense of responsibility when my predecessor handed me the keys to Brooklyn Union. This was a very special company, and I wanted to not only preserve its unique character but add a few touches of my own that might just result in something lasting and valuable. One thing is certain: I am the only CEO in the company's history to promote an ex-monk, a move that probably raised some eyebrows but has paid more dividends than I ever could have imagined.

I know that I am not the best or the smartest CEO to be found and certainly not the highest-paid or best-known in the business press. I have made plenty of mistakes along the way. But I do feel extremely comfortable that I will leave behind a very clear set of beliefs about the ethical way to conduct business and treat people. I made that easy for myself by following a fairly simple but rigid set of values and principles from the very beginning of my career, values that came as much from the company as from me. Such a point of view may not be very exciting or newsworthy, but it certainly helped me find my way through more than four decades of my working life. It also made it easier to sleep well at night.

So in that vein, a crucial mandate for me is to feel as certain as is reasonably possible that I can pass along the values and beliefs about people that are integral to this culture. Once I am gone, I am only "the former CEO" of KeySpan, and I will have little or no influence on the future of the company. But my fervent hope is that my successor embraces the true nature of this company and its people and makes that a fundamental part of his or her agenda. In that way, my legacy will live on.

I don't know if my successor will choose to work with Kenny the way I have, but I certainly will urge him or her to. In a business environment fraught with uncertainty, having access to a calm, patient, insightful, unbiased, and spiritual point of view is invaluable. I have always believed that though Kenny's monastic background was not a job requirement, it has clearly been a significant benefit for me and the company. A touch of divine grace—secular and nondenominational—is a welcome guest in these troubled times. As Polaroid founder Edwin Land once said, "The bottom line is in heaven."

It is not a simple matter to transfer your ex-monk on to your successor. My relationship with Kenny is a special one, perhaps nontransferable. It is built on a business foundation, but it is a very personal relationship. Kenny and I sit alone, just the two of us, and talk about company matters in a way that transcends the usual business discussion. We say things to each other that people probably couldn't say unless they had strong feelings of confidence and trust in each other. These conversations are frank and honest but intently focused on the common good of the organization. He tells me the bad news with the same equanimity as the good. He makes suggestions based not on a personal agenda but on a compassionate wisdom about people and how they are feeling. With Kenny keeping me in touch with the real voice of the company, I never get isolated in an ivory tower, as many CEOs do. Whether or not you can assign that relationship over to someone else is hard to say. If anybody could inspire that trust, however, it is Kenny.

But I'm not fooling myself here. I have a very realistic view of how treacherous the road ahead is. My successor will not only inherit an amazing company and a world-class group of people, but he or she will also be faced with a daunting array of tough questions and few easy answers. I believe we are in the midst of a tectonic shift in business. And because we are smack in the center of such dramatic change, it is almost impossible to get a clear view of where to go and how to get there.

The global economic and geopolitical forces that have pounded away at all of our existing notions of strategy and execution over the past few years have taken a toll. The ramifications of 9/11 are still being felt and probably will be for some time to come. It isn't clear anymore who the winners and losers are going to be. Some corporate giants that dominated the marketplace just a few short years ago are shells of their former selves or no longer exist today. Many very smart people are out of work or struggling to rebuild shattered careers. Some are working with defense attorneys to avoid jail sentences for corporate malfeasance. We have had graphic lessons on how to do things wrong and very few examples of best practices that will work in this daunting business environment.

But one thing I am sure about: Doing the right thing, being socially responsible, and holding tightly to a core set of values about how to do business and how to treat people will never go out of fashion. I have always believed, in my heart of hearts, that if you do good out there, you will be recognized for it. Knowing that KeySpan makes a difference for its employees, for its customers, and out in the community while still achieving its business goals illustrates to me that the concept of enlightened self-interest is more appropriate today than at any time in business history. If my successor understands this, everything else he or she accomplishes will be built on this foundation.

So as I work with the board to identify my successor, I focus on what I believe are two essential requirements: an ability to implement a strategy and vision that will take advantage of a far more deregulated and competitive energy industry, and the emotional intelligence and integrity to never lose sight of the soul of the organization.

My vision has always been for KeySpan to become the premier energy company in the Northeast. I am not sure you ever really attain your vision completely. But we have certainly become a premier energy company in the Northeast. Given where we were in 1991 and where we are today, in terms of profits, growth, and shareholder value, I feel quite proud of those achievements. KeySpan is now a profitable Fortune 500 corporation well positioned for future success in its core businesses.

What truly satisfies me is that we have done this while holding firmly to our core values and not compromising the spiritual center of the company in order to attain our financial goals. We have accomplished as much in terms of social responsibility as fiscal responsibility. Whether it is establishing funds to help low-income families pay their fuel bills or promoting environmentally sound applications of natural gas for vehicles, I have always pushed the company to go the extra mile beyond what was required.

Sometimes my people have gotten annoyed with me for committing to causes when there is no money in the budget and I have simply told them to find a way to do it. Other times, the focus has been on whether we can have a big KeySpan banner in the picture so that we get a branding opportunity from our involvement in a cause. That's nice if you can get it, but it goes much deeper than that. We have gone out into the community and done the good works that not only established a positive glow to our brand but allowed our people to do the right thing and feel proud that they worked for KeySpan. No numeric value can be put on that. It is priceless.

So choosing a successor may well be the most important thing that I do. If you believe, as I do, that a corporation is a living entity, it must be cared for, nourished, nurtured, and protected as it grows. The person who succeeds me is inheriting not just a public company but a public trust. In that arena, his or her job will be harder than mine. The result of doing good for so long is that much is expected from a lot of constituencies. The phone at the KeySpan Foundation never stops ringing. The disastrous stock market has diminished the investments that provide for our contributions, so there simply isn't as much to go around. Because most of these organizations have seen their support from all sources drastically eroded, the decisions become more wrenching for us. But it is in the tough times that you get tested. We can't just look at it strictly from a business standpoint, because there is more to it than that. And in the long run, I am convinced such community involvement helps the business.

People have told me that I cast a long shadow. I'm not sure I could receive a nicer compliment. Yet I am wary of taking such comments too seriously. I recently attended a fund-raising event for the Brooklyn Academy of Music. They asked a few of us from the Brooklyn Economic Development Group to come and make a sales pitch on behalf of the Academy. As I was leaving, one of the Academy's administrators came over and said, "Bob, I don't know what we're going to do when you leave. You are such a force in Brooklyn and everybody respects you so much. You're the one we look to when we have gatherings like this." Needless to say, I was very flattered. But in quiet moments, I realize that what really gives me the ability to do a lot of what I do is that I am the CEO of KeySpan. Once I step down, I won't have that platform from which to operate. I plan to stay involved in the community. I just hope that they will still think I'm a nice guy.

To be honest, I am not one of those CEOs who will have to be carried out of the building, kicking and screaming. I love what I do and I am sure I could go on for quite a while if I had to. But I'm also certain that new blood is good for an organization, especially an old utility like ours. I've heard some criticism now and then about how I have handled the succession efforts. It goes with the territory. Herbert Bayard Swope said, "I cannot give you a formula for success, but I can give you a formula for failure: try to please everybody."

As a consensus builder, I know firsthand how true that is. Whomever we choose to succeed me, it will leave somebody disgruntled. The good news is that as important as the CEO may be, he or she cannot do it alone. I've spent a great deal of time building an extremely strong management team at KeySpan. I've worked hard to bring in high-level outside talent to balance our homegrown veterans. Knowing this team is in place makes my departure easier to accept.

The board, including myself, indulged in some healthy debate over the past two years about a successor. Some felt I had waited too long to address this issue. Others thought we had to bring in someone from the outside to inspire a fresh and more global focus for the company as it moved into the future. The board extended my contract to provide more time to groom a successor. At the same time, we identified two internal candidates and positioned them as the leading contenders for the job. We gave them each a great deal of responsibility so that we could evaluate which one will likely succeed me.

That created some controversy. People see it now as a horse race and try to pick the winner. They try to align themselves with that person, and it has upped the internal politics in a way that I would have preferred to avoid. We thought long and hard about going outside to find someone new, but even if that remains a possibility until we actually name someone, my preference is to promote from within. Many companies have successfully gone outside for a new leader. Fresh, new points of view and leadership style can be inspiring.

But we felt that with the culture at KeySpan, we had too much at risk to venture that far into the unknown. What we have created here at KeySpan is meaningful and it has worked. We want to maintain that, protect that, going forward. We might not feel that the internal candidates have all of the skills at this moment that they will need to be the CEO, but we know they have grown up within our culture and they understand and believe in the values we've built the company upon.

One thing I learned quickly was that you really never know the CEO job until you put on the shoes and see how it feels. My journey in these shoes has been both inspiring and humbling. I never would have believed that a kid from the streets of Brooklyn could have experienced all this and walked where I have walked.

In his book *The Hero's Farewell: What Happens When CEOs Retire* (Oxford University Press, 1988), Jeffrey Sonnenfeld wrote that within their organizations CEOs become folk heroes. And like mythic heroes, business heroes "not only symbolize dreams and aspirations to their firms, and even to general society, but also are accomplishers of pragmatic goals."

I have never thought of myself as a folk hero—or any kind of hero, for that matter. It is wonderful if I've been able to symbolize the dreams and aspirations of KeySpan. If I did, it was only because I paid close attention to the pragmatic goals . . . and the corporate soul.

The Monk

~

Not long ago, I had lunch with Lenore Puleo, one of our executive officers. Lenore is in charge of our client services area, and she was interested in dramatically improving the way her people performed their work. She had been to a presentation by Tony Robbins, the self-help guru, and she came back excited about the idea of self-generated transformation.

What she did is emblematic of the KeySpan culture. She gathered her leadership team together and told them they were going to design and implement an entirely new course. Not only would all 2,000 of the client services employees take the course, but it would be created by her team, who would teach it to the managers, who would then teach everyone else in the organization.

At lunch, Lenore told me she was getting some backlash from her people who thought she was overly bold with her concept. She said to me, "Kenny, I want to do this, but I'm worried that I'm going off the deep end. Maybe I'm going too far. I understand leadership and you are only a leader as long as people want to follow you. When they stop following you, you are in trouble. I don't want to cross that line."

Her plan was extremely ambitious and maybe just a bit crazy. But she also had an obvious passion for it. "I feel strongly that this is the right thing for the business," she told me, "but I'm concerned that I'm moving too fast." My time in the monastery taught me that the old cliché "Nothing ventured, nothing gained" has real truth to it. I said to Lenore, "If you feel it's good for the business and you have passion around it, I'd recommend you push forward. Don't be deterred."

Afterward, I sent her a note of encouragement, quoting the writer Harold Whitman: "Don't ask yourself what the world needs, ask yourself what makes you come alive. And then go do that. Because what the world needs are people who have come alive."

Lenore told me later that my support was just what she needed to propel her forward, a small but significant push that allowed her to leap ahead despite her fears. She even framed the quote and hung it outside her office, where it still resides today.

What she created was astounding. The program, which was transformational not only for the business but also for the employees who have participated in it, was a tremendous success.

She calls the program the Client Services Competitive Edge Workshop. Nearly every one of the 2,000 client services people has participated in the workshop, and they have rated it the best workshop they have ever had at KeySpan. By designing it and having KeySpan people teach it, the company has saved more than $1 million in costs.

Essentially, the workshop is focused on improving communications skills and working more effectively with internal clients. But it has turned out to be more powerful than that. According to Lenore, the core of the course is to teach people how to shift from negative feelings to positive ones by changing how they move and react and what they do in certain situations. It is, at its essence, a spiritual experience in that it taps into the power within people to take control of their own emotions in the course of their daily work lives. Though not everyone becomes a convert, most have embraced the concept so enthusiastically that it has changed their lives, both inside and outside work.

Not only did KeySpan endorse the program, but Craig Matthews, before he retired in 2002, showed up one day, stepped into a workshop room, and was overwhelmed by the noise, the enthusiasm, the loud music, the glow lights around people's necks. He carried with him a string of plastic frogs that he'd kept in his office. He told Lenore's group that he gave out these frogs—he called it the Leap Frog Award—to people who have made quantum leap improvements in their work.

I would guess that most companies, especially utilities, would find such a program unwelcome and frightening. But here, we find ways to embrace the unknown. Lenore said to me, "What other company could I do this in and feel not only that I could get away with it, but that it would be encouraged with a loud 'Bravo!' "

For me, this incident serves as a small example of my work with KeySpan. My responsibility is often about nurturing and encouraging the talents of others. It's also about connecting their personal passion to the needs of the business. In some regards, I serve as a type of midwife for the company. I remember listening to an interview with a famous midwife, and the reporter asked this seasoned veteran of birthing: "How many babies have you delivered in your lifetime?" Her answer was clear and to the point: "I don't deliver babies. Mothers do. I *catch* them!"

That's often how I feel about my role in the company. I am not financially astute or operationally adept. But maybe I don't need to be. We have many employees whose skills and capabilities go far beyond what I could offer. My role is to help foster the environment for their skills and gifts to be offered, as well as captured. I don't create that talent, I simply help nurture it and ensure that their gifts get "caught" and utilized for the betterment of the business.

Since I come from a vastly different tradition, I also have the ability to contribute to the business in nontraditional and inviting ways— not necessarily in religious ways, but certainly in spiritual ones. What I do is find ways to reflect the innate sacredness of employees' talents, gifts, and God-given capabilities. I've tried to use creative ways to engage the vast store of abilities that workers bring daily to their jobs, ways that less enlightened employers fail to capitalize upon. My gift is in recognizing this creativity and connecting it to the values and goals of the business. I also have a knack for inviting executives into the process so that the talents of our employees get directly connected to the business needs. Then, lastly, I get myself out of the way.

This is my offering. It is part of Bob's insight that he recognized and encouraged me and integrated my skills into the workings of the business.

The job of a CEO is getting more challenging all the time. Some might even say it has become overwhelming. Rapidly changing markets, the demands from Wall Street, and the necessity of meeting short-term goals while maintaining long-term strategies make a CEO's role daunting in ways that are hard to quantify. While even God had a chance to rest at the end of the week, the CEO of today doesn't seem to get that luxury. The work has become so all-encompassing that today's business leaders will take help from anyone willing to offer it. Even that of a monk. And I've felt privileged for being given the opportunity to contribute.

Looking at KeySpan's future, one of the challenges before us is maintaining employee loyalty in the midst of a changing economy. While loyalty may seem to be out-of-date in this current environment, to me it is more important than ever. Certainly the concept needs work, a renewed examination of what it means and how it can be attained under difficult conditions. But it simply can't be ignored. Loyalty matters, especially in a world where so many feel alienated and alone. Money and corporate perks are valuable and necessary, but ultimately inadequate for engaging the commitment of workers. We need to continue to struggle with finding ways to engage the vast expanse of potential that lies within the soul of each person who walks into the company.

We must also continue to find new ways for connecting the talents of employees to the needs of the business. I am encouraged to see the growing number of co-workers who have a natural and professional way for making this happen.

As a poet and painter, I would also like to make the workplace friendlier for artists. We can't rely solely on accountants and engineers to safeguard our corporate institutions. We need artists to complement their efforts. Artists have the sensitivity and skills for building the spiritual side of business. In large part, it is the voice of the artist that has remained silent during recent corporate failures. It is they, however, who are the shamans of the twenty-first century.

Some business and religious leaders have left us feeling violated and without hope. We need spokespeople for the sacred and the true, which coexist within the world of commerce. Our organizational charts long for those who can use word, color, and brush to reveal that the world has became surprisingly small and that an individual's action reverberates across the globe. Artists remind us that misdeeds done by a few can injure the many. Just as we look to our internal "adult" for moral direction, we should look externally to the poets, painters, and mystics in our places of work to shore up the frailty of the human condition in the marketplace.

We all have a vocation, and it is not independent from our need to earn a living. My stint in the business world has taught me that you don't need to go to a monastery to develop yourself spiritually. All you need to do is get a job and go off to work. It forces us to show up, take risks, and deal with our own imperfections. It is no small task to be living examples for good in a business world that doesn't always support it. The Divine bestows a multiplicity of talents upon us all and they are given in service of the world, not just ourselves. Work winds up being a wonderful place to get them used, be of service to others, as well as make some money—all in the same day.

The Divine's will is often revealed in the context of community with others and in using our God-given talents to make the world better. Bosses, co-workers, and the economy will provide us with more than ample opportunities to practice kindness, forgiveness, and a note of hope to a sometimes beleaguered world.

My future is clear, to the extent anything ever is. I will continue to use my skills to engage the passion and energy that is already in the company. To the degree that I can continue to work with senior management in identifying and meeting business needs—and do that in a way that engages the talents of our employees—I expect to remain gainfully employed. And as long as the good Lord continues to place people like Bob Catell in my life who make it possible for me to contribute, I look forward to staying on.

My two near-death experiences offered me the deep realization that my place in the world, as well as in the workplace, is never a certain thing. In many regards, it's not all that different for me than for anybody else. Monasticism has taught me that we are all just "temporary" workers anyway. We should spend our time wisely and well because there are no guarantees.

At the end of my life's work, my final wish is to arrive at the same place as Sir Thomas More, that noble lawyer, saint, and astute businessman. He met his Maker with the clarity of a well-seasoned man of the world: "I die the king's good servant, but God's first."

My wish is to make that final journey with that same sense of clarity and faith.

Epilogue

The CEO

When I think of my mother, a quote comes to mind from Calvin Ellis Stowe: "Common sense is the knack of seeing things as they are, and doing things as they ought to be done." For me, this is the spiritual context of life. This is not something a parent can instill in a child through words; it is passed along with the habits of a daily life lived in a certain way. I know that I learned this from her as a child in Brooklyn and it took root and grew along with me through my life and my career.

My mother taught me to believe in God. She taught me to respect people and to do good on this earth while you are here. I really believe in that. If you ask whether people have a soul and the soul lives on after we die, I do not know the answer to that, and to be honest, I don't think about it very much. But I do believe in God. I pray. I try to live a decent life treating people with respect and honesty and caring.

I'm not sure that many young business executives climbing their own corporate ladders would embrace such an ideology as the catalyst for a successful career these days. The message from far too many CEOs has centered around massive compensation packages, aggressive take-no-prisoners business strategies, and questionable accounting of a company's true value.

It's not a surprise therefore that the public is widely disillusioned about American business. History is unlikely to record the past several years as a renaissance in corporate America. But it might prove to be the quiet beginning of a new era in social responsibility and enlightened self-interest. At least, that's what I hope will be the case. The way the business community rallied together in New York City after 9/11 demonstrated an incredible ability to rise to the nation's call and put social responsibility above all else. I would hope that as time passes, this focus on the common good doesn't fade into memory.

I certainly do not profess to hold the key to progressive business doctrine. I am certain that I have made enough mistakes in my tenure as CEO to disqualify myself from any pantheons of corporate wisdom. And I will be the first to admit that the bigger an organization becomes, the more difficult it is to maintain the kind of corporate values that KeySpan has always espoused. It isn't enough to be socially responsible if you are not providing shareholder value and inspiring confidence in your company. At the same time, using growth and expansion as an excuse for abandoning your core moral beliefs is unacceptable.

As my corporate journey winds down, I believe that I was able to accomplish quite a lot by holding to the kind of values that allow a company to achieve both profit and purpose. If that is out-of-date and old-fashioned, then maybe I am going to retire at the right time. However, I simply don't believe that. The kind of environment that would allow someone like Kenny Moore to emerge as a significant influence on our corporate consciousness is worth a hard look. While KeySpan seeks the highest profits and shareholder value, it continues to aim toward what I call our true north. Having a moral compass, to me, is as important as positive cash flow.

We have no corner on the market for this kind of thinking. Countless companies, across every industry, embrace our way of doing business, each with its own style and grace. I remember in December 1995 when Malden Mills, a company in Lawrence, Massachusetts, suffered a devastating fire. The CEO, Aaron Feuerstein, stood in the parking lot and watched as three of the company's buildings burned and said, "This is not the end." He decided immediately to continue to pay his 3,000 workers full salaries and benefits over the next three months as the company struggled to survive. This cost him millions of dollars, but he never hesitated to do what he felt was the right thing. He said, "The fundamental difference is that I consider our workers an asset, not an expense."

Most of the good works of CEOs and their companies are far less dramatic but no less meaningful. Unfortunately, perhaps, it doesn't make for good copy so the media tends to ignore these stories. In an era of corporate downsizing and massive layoffs, Feuerstein emerged as a hero. He believed he was only doing the right thing. His spiritual response, which he insisted had as much to do with good business sense as moral duty, is odd only in that it stands out so dramatically against what most people perceive to be the cold indifference of modern business.

When you have been at something for more than 45 years, you often get asked about the secret to your success and longevity. Though we never intended this book to be a how-to guide, the process of writing it has forced me to consider some of the lessons I have learned through this journey.

I honestly feel deep gratitude for what our people do, everyday, sometimes under the harshest conditions, with military-like precision. They honor the company and themselves, and it reflects everything about what we are and what we believe in. KeySpan has an outstanding safety record. We measure people's incentive bonuses by customer satisfaction surveys. In other words, we take all this very seriously. And I feel very humbled by what they accomplish and achieve. In a world where corporate loyalty is essentially a thing of the past, it is rejuvenating to witness the passion KeySpan people bring to their jobs and to the community.

So while I am flattered when people refer to my honesty and integrity, the truth is that it all stems from the feelings I have about our people. I am simply incapable of undermining what they do and what they have built by behaving in a questionable or unethical manner. It is just too valuable a trust to risk.

Maybe the best thing I have done is not take myself too seriously. No matter how high I've climbed in the corporate world, I'm still just a Brooklyn kid. If I tried to put on airs, everybody would know I was a phony. I'm more comfortable sitting in the crowd at a ballgame than I am hobnobbing with celebrities or business tycoons. In fact, I've had season tickets to my favorite sports team, the New York Rangers, since 1986, and they are not down near the ice with the corporate honchos in suits but up in the blue seats where the real hockey fans sit.

For years, I would go to games after work with my son. I never wore my suit and tie because you just didn't dress up in the blue seats. When you have season tickets, you get to know the people around you pretty well. You and they become a regular group. And they all knew me as Bob Catell and that I worked for the gas company. But I never said anything more about it. Then, in 1996, after we had taken on the KeySpan name for our holding company, the marketing people ran a full-page add in the local newspapers featuring a picture of me with the caption, "Bob Catell, chairman and CEO of KeySpan."

I got a call in my office that day from one of my hockey buddies whom I had known for years. He started yelling, "Catell, you son of a bitch. You never told us you were the CEO!" I laughed and told him I didn't think that mattered at a hockey game. He said, "Yeah, true. But from now on, you can buy the beer."

Here are some other lessons I've learned along the way:

- I have always avoided corporate politics and worked hard. That may sound corny, but my theory has always been that if you work hard and do the best job you can whether you love the job or not, you will get recognized for it and rewarded with opportunity. I never worried about the politics or lobbied for a specific job. And I don't think I've ever complained about my job, even when I was out digging trenches in the streets of Brooklyn on the hottest August day.

- I am a voracious reader, and that has helped me stay abreast of what is going on in the energy industry and in the world. Even when we were a little gas company in Brooklyn, I felt it was important to know what was happening in the global energy arena. You can never know too much.

- The most important reason for my success is having a sensitivity to people at all levels of the company. Whether someone is a union worker in the operations area or a senior executive, I treat people the same. Being sensitive to people's needs, liking people, being willing to listen to people's views, and respecting people have gotten me through many rough spots over the years.

- Building consensus is worth the effort. I am aware that some people question my toughness and whether or not I'm as hard-nosed as one needs to be in business. I feel that I'm quite capable of making tough decisions. The buck stops with me. But I try to build consensus and have people on board with my decisions. That's not always possible, but when it is, things tend to work much better.

- My time with my family is vitally important. I'm sure some who know me will chuckle at this because I tend to work from 6 A.M. to 10 P.M. five days a week. Between work itself and the external demands, there are few hours left in my days. But I have always saved my weekends for quiet time with my family, away from the job. My wife has been incredibly understanding and supportive. My five children are all grown now, but when they were young and I was working all the time, I believed it was important to build relationships with each of them. I wanted to let them know that I'm there for them and that no matter how much I achieve in my professional life, I'm still their father.

- I am intensely loyal. It is undoubtedly difficult to find a lot of 45-year company veterans in corporate America anymore. People focus so intently on the financial rewards and their next career move that the idea of corporate loyalty is just about obsolete. To me, that is a shame. I understand that this is a two-way street and American workers have been burned by downsizing and massive layoffs, especially during this dismal economy. But there is great satisfaction in sticking to something you feel is important and creating something valuable in that way.

Just as I never dreamed that I would one day become the CEO of a major corporation, I also never imagined that I would find myself working side by side with a former monk. I'll never know for certain why our paths crossed or why our relationship jelled and allowed us to create this unique partnership. But one thing I've learned over the course of my career is that you don't stop to question the unexpected gifts you receive along the way that help you do a better job.

Kenny's sage counsel and reasoned insight have indeed been a gift. But more than that, he has offered me a wonderful lens through which to view the company and the world around it. He taught me to accept the never-ending feedback from my constituencies with an open mind and heart.

There is indeed a spiritual side to business, a soul within the company. I believe there is more to what we do than just business. Kenny has often talked about the passion and creativity of our people, and that is something I've invested in. I don't think I could have succeeded any other way.

The Monk

~

The Gospels remind us that there remains something sacred about the world of business and those that live out their vocation there. Spirituality at work isn't about hosting prayer groups or Bible study sessions in the workplace. I don't think the business world is ready for that, and I'm not sure it should be.

The separation of church and state continues to be a viable model in such a diverse world. I believe that the Divine is more interested in having us acknowledge our God-given talents and using them for the betterment of others and ourselves. There's something inherently holy about embarking on that effort.

I have spent numerous years working in large hierarchical institutions, 20 of them in a corporate setting and 15 in a monastery. Whenever you are dealing with large numbers of people joined together around a singular effort, many of the operating principles seem to feel oddly similar. The media once asked Pope John XXIII how many people worked at the Vatican. "About half of them," he said. It's funny how the challenges confronting leaders, religious and secular alike, have some universal qualities.

Having sojourned in two dominant institutional structures throughout the years, here are some of the salient points that stay with me:

- Remember that most people are doing the best they can. When I worked in the monastery, 10 percent of the people I met were saints; 10 percent were self-serving rascals; 80 percent were just ordinary folks trying to make improvements to an inherently flawed human system. I found the same ratio when I joined corporate life. It's remarkable how people still continue to show up with a sense of passion and commitment for the work. They deserve our compassion and support. More importantly, they warrant our companionship. Nobody should have to endure the vicissitudes of life alone. It's surprising to see how much fun it actually can be when we make the journey together.

- Keep your head in the clouds, but your feet firmly planted on the ground. The business world abhors idealists who speak lovely words but accomplish little. It delights in folks with enthusiasm who are committed to accomplishing a tangible result. People of integrity who are committed to a business purpose give me hope for a better tomorrow.

- Don't focus only on high-potential employees; also pay attention to your average ones. They perform most of the work anyway. Engaging their ardor is the key to corporate excellence. I'd even recommend spending some time with the poor performers. I think there are wonderful economies of scale there. Further inducements to an already high achiever get you little. But motivating a laggard dramatically improves operations. Somebody once said that idleness and indifference are proper responses to meaningless work. Perhaps dawdlers are prognosticators of corporate renewal in disguise. Those living on the margins of any social group can teach us a lot. All prophets for change come from the margins of the community. Maybe that is why the divine usually shows up first amidst folks who are relegated to live there.

- Become a better communicator by keeping your mouth shut. Listening has become a lost art in business. We risk creating a culture where the ones that speak the most and the loudest win out. My instincts tell me that that's not going to satisfy our customers, whether external or internal. There is something to be said for maintaining a quiet demeanor. Silence on our part invites the thoughts and opinions of others, a true recipe for sustained growth and competitive advantage.

- Increase your tolerance for opinions that drive you wacky. The future never arrives as we expect; it's always a surprise. Anytime the Divine showed up in the world, most of the folks totally missed the event. They were expecting something more conventional. We risk making the same mistake in business. Breakthroughs show up as irritating distractions to defined business plans. Discordant voices and questioning personalities are harbingers of niche markets and need to be encouraged. Expanding our comfort with surprise leads us to new lines of business. It's also one of the few practical steps we can take to prepare for heaven.

- Remember to occasionally say a prayer. Working out in the world is too tough to go it alone. Spend some time asking for assistance. Prayer also helps that much needed business skill: humility. Success, both personal and corporate, is largely dependent on people and things outside our control. Periodically offering a humble prayer is simply acknowledging that. Napoleon was onto something when he said that leaders are brokers in hope. The work of an executive seems largely spiritual to me: building trust, inspiring staff, gaining commitment, and offering hope. You would be foolish not to ask for all the help you can get.

And a last bit of advice: Don't go out and hire a monk to work for your company. You don't need one. Rather, use the employees you already have. They are the ones who know the business, care about the product, and have a vested interest in making it all work out profitably. Engaging their enthusiasm will be enough to capture the Divine's fancy and get you all the blessings needed for success.

The journalist Eric Sevareid once said that he was a pessimist about tomorrow but an optimist about the day after tomorrow. I feel the same way about business. I don't expect corporate malfeasance to end anytime in the near future. The workplace is a mirror of life. Like it or not, evil is part of the human condition and will always exist in the world. Besides, if immorality were to suddenly come to an abrupt halt, much of life's drama would be lost and organized religion would be out of a job. And as all MBAs know, losing jobs is never good for the economy.

The Divine's invitation to us is to get in there and be a player as the drama unfolds. Using our hands, heads, and hearts in service of something larger than ourselves is what's required. Business has tremendous potential to be a force for good in the world. While it hasn't always lived up to this challenge, the opportunity remains ever present. We who labor there have direct influence on the outcome. And our impact has the potential to be dramatic.

Some might balk at the impossibility of effectively nurturing the spiritual within the commercial. And for these people, I have a compassionate understanding of this challenge. However, one of the things I learned in the monastery was that just because something appears impossible doesn't mean you don't need to work on it. (Why else would I have been required to take the vow of celibacy?)

Some of what we are required to work on will not be accomplished in our lifetimes. That's what vision, brilliance, and legacy are about. To those needing encouragement, I give you the words of Father Theodore, my old religious adviser: "If you think you're too small to be effective, then you've never been in bed with a mosquito." We all can have an impact, even if it's a small one.

The poet Theodore Roethke said it well: "What we need is more people who specialize in the impossible." The challenges are formidable, yet the need is great. Life invites us daily to take the risk and act on making the impossible happen. That is at the heart of what makes showing up for work so exciting.

Acknowledgments

*W*e would like to thank the following people who helped make the creation of this book possible.

The book would not have come to life without the undaunted determination of David Manning, the visionary support of Arden Melick, and personal dedication of Kathy Ambery. We are deeply beholden to Peter Osgood, Steve Zelkowitz, Elaine Weinstein, Fred Lowther, Neil Nichols, Mary Cardillo, Maurice Shaw, Ron Macklin, David Elliott, Loretta Smith, Nick Stavropoulos, Ken Daly, Lynne Forte, Don Bosco, and Lyn Maxner for their steadfast support. We also want to thank Robert E. Murphy for his excellent history of Brooklyn Union, which provided a wealth of insight about the company. Our thanks go as well to Larry Alexander and Paula Sinnott at John Wiley & Sons, for helping bring our vision to fruition.

Bob would like to express his deep love and gratitude to his wife Joan and his children, Robert, Carla, Donna, Laura, and Erica, for their incredible support and love throughout his long and rewarding career. Without them, this book would not have come to life. "And a special thanks to my sister Padma, who taught me so much about people and who is my dear friend."

Kenny is likewise indebted to his mentor, Shelli Kanet, and his sage literary adviser, Alexis Harley. "My efforts would not have been possible without the support of my family; the pestering of my sons, Christopher and Matthew, and the encouragement of my beloved in-laws, Enrica and Tony Presto."

Glenn Rifkin offers his love and gratitude to his family: Janie, Ben, Cameron, and Laura, and to his mother Lillian.

A final word of deep gratitude goes to the officers and employees of KeySpan who have inspired us with their personal passion and professional commitment to business and the world.

Index